'Anyone seeking knowledge and union with God will be informed, edified, nourished and utterly charmed by this book. I savoured every story and was nurtured by the expression and depth. It is a book absolutely after my own heart.'

Anne Lamott, author of Traveling Mercies
and Small Victories

'One thing is for sure, there are no cheap and easy answers to why our experiences can be maddeningly painful, deeply disappointing and feel like we are wrestling with darkness. However, Mark Yaconelli's book will help you to feel safe to ask why. Through a powerful use of stories, he helps us to see beyond comfortable answers to find that Jesus is on the same road as we are, so we too, like him, can move forward.'

Russ Parker, author of Free to Fail
and Healing Wounded History

'I am undone. Maybe it's because Mark Yaconelli is the best storyteller of his generation or because these pages are so achingly honest or because somehow this guy just has my number – but whatever the reason, this book made me softer, more open, more human. This is a book of dazzling grace, a slice of holy ground, as life-giving as water in the desert. Take your shoes off and drink up.'

Kenda Dean, Professor of Youth, Church, and Culture,
Princeton Theological Seminary and
author of Almost Christian

'Mark knows how to tell stories and share ideas that pull at the soul. He writes about faith in a way that makes perfect, comforting sense while taking us to often uncomfortable new places. This constantly surprising, intricately constructed book is a gift to anyone who has ever sat and wondered at the profoundly, heartbreakingly, tragically beautiful nature of life, and asked: "How on earth do I make sense of it all?" Mark might not have all the answers, but he makes a fine travelling companion as we wrestle with the biggest questions of all.'

Martin Saunders, Contributing Editor, Christian Today
and author of The Beautiful Disciplines

DISAPPOINTMENT, DOUBT and other SPIRITUAL GIFTS

MARK YACONELLI

Originally published in the United States of America in 2016
as *The Gift of Hard Things* by
InterVarsity Press, Downers Grove, Illinois

First published in Great Britain in 2016

Society for Promoting Christian Knowledge
36 Causton Street
London SW1P 4ST
www.spck.org.uk

Chapter 2, "Prayer Service Disaster", first appeared as "The Gift of Spiritual Poverty", *Premier Youthwork*, September 2010.
Sections of chapter 3, "Idiots", first appeared in "Lessons from a Holy Man", *Premier Youthwork*, July 2015.
Chapter 6, "Initiation", first appeared in "Initiation", *Immerse Journal*, November–December 2011.
Sections of chapter 7, "The Ungrieved Grief", first appeared as "The Ministry of Grief", *Premier Youthwork*, November 2011.
Sections of chapter 9, "The Dark Night", first appeared in "Ministry Through the Dark Night", *Premier Christianity*, June 2014.

British Library Cataloguing-in-Publication Data
A catalogue record for this book is available from the British Library

ISBN 978–0–281–07650–5
eBook ISBN 978–0–281–07651–2

Manufacture managed by Jellyfish
First printed in Great Britain by CPI
Subsequently digitally printed in Great Britain

eBook by Graphicraft Limited, Hong Kong

Produced on paper from sustainable forests

For Jill,

through sorrow or joy,

in hardship or in ease,

I am yours.

Contents

About the Author

Mark Yaconelli is a writer, speaker, spiritual director, retreat leader, community activist and storyteller. He is the founder and executive director of The Hearth Community, a registered non-profit organization that assists cities and charitable agencies in producing personal storytelling projects. He is the author of numerous books including *Contemplative Youth Ministry, Growing Souls* and *Wonder, Fear and Longing* (all published by SPCK). Mark lives in southern Oregon, USA, with his wife Jill and their three children.

Introduction

The Alchemy of Grace

I love the thing that I most
wish had not happened.

Stephen Colbert

One April afternoon I sat in the backyard of a nineteenth-century farm house with my friend Eric watching our two ten-year-old daughters run and play across a green meadow dotted with wildflowers. Enjoying the smell of apple blossoms, the late afternoon light and cold iced tea, we became engaged in conversation and lost track of our daughters. Thirty minutes went by until Eric's wife called from the house, "Where are the girls?"

Chagrined, we stood suddenly and scanned the field. To our surprise we spotted the girls atop two horses, riding along the far perimeter of the meadow. Eric did not own horses. Our daughters had no equine experience. Quickly, and without a word to Eric's wife, we ran across the field where we spotted a woman in Wranglers and a straw cowboy hat standing in the shadow of an oak grove, shouting instructions to our daughters.

Her name was Jane and she worked a ranch up in the Green Springs Mountain area above our valley. She had rights to bring her horses down to the hundred-acre meadow for fresh grass, water and "to stimulate their minds and hearts." Jane called herself a "horse shrink"—a therapist for horses. She took in abandoned and abused animals, brought them back to their natural selves and then sold them to caring owners. We stood in the shade of the black oaks as Jane told us about her work. "Sometimes I get horses who have spent their whole lives cooped up in a barn. Since birth they have lived in darkness, eating from an oat bucket, drinking from a trough. They've never seen the world, never had fresh water from a creek or eaten grass in a field or had space to run in the open. When I'm given one of these horses I bring it down here to this meadow for a week or so. I set up a camping trailer and just let it go free."

"What happens?" I asked.

"Well, the first day and night it stays next to my trailer whining for oats and water. Here it has over a hundred acres of green grass, and it stares at me like it's starving, begging for food."

"Do you feed it?"

"No. I walk it to the creek or take it out to the middle of the meadow, and still it whines and begs. Sometimes it stands in the creek, with water running over its hooves, crying with thirst! It is so routinized to buckets and troughs that it doesn't recognize anything, even when its nose smells water.

"And then, out of sheer desperation, the horse will bow its head and brush its lips along the creek and stick out its tongue, and then suddenly drink and toss its head and whinny with happiness. And a day later, because it's half-starved, it will reach down into the meadow and tear up a clump of grass and eat. Then, all of a sudden, it knows. *I am surrounded by food!*"

Jane laughed.

"What happens when the realization hits?" I wondered.

"It runs. The horse will take off and gallop and kick and run. That's the moment I love most. That's why I do this work. To see that moment when a creature realizes it's free within a big beautiful world. That's pure joy."

Standing at the edge of the meadow I felt I was hearing a parable for my own life. The horse's experience was all too familiar: The safe, restricted, unending life of routine and predictability. The unexpected (and unwanted) disruption and accompanying fear. The overwhelming despair and grief at the loss of the familiar. The fixating on the past. The distress that blinds one to surrounding possibilities. The shock of joy when you realize that beneath the suffering lies verdant fields of life and freedom.

Watching my daughter atop that black horse striding calmly through the green grass, I had a deep awareness that one of the invitations in this life is to hold confusion, frustration and suffering as possibility. If only I could loosen my own expectations (of self, others, God) and embrace moments of disappointment and doubt, I might discover a field of green. It's not that we ought to look for suffering, but if it should find us there is a truth that life's hardships, if we're able to accept them, often contain unexpected gifts.

Of course, this is a recurring insight that I struggle to embrace. As a white, middle-class Westerner, I have been taught that the pursuit and realization of my individual desires and appetites are my birthright. I have been taught that with discipline, planning and hard work, life will conform to my expectations. Our society doesn't tolerate the idea that we (individually and collectively) lack control. Even in our spiritual lives we hold up teachers, books and spiritual practices that promise happiness, peace and health. And yet is there anything more destructive than human beings who believe they have life under control? Under this illusion we assume our every fortune is earned and every suffering deserved. How isolating.

We need to cultivate an ongoing awareness that we are small, sensitive creatures with short lifespans in a world that is often chaotic, capricious, mysterious, terrible and wonderful all at the same time. Failure, disappointment, loss and other difficult experiences call us to accept our humanity, feel grateful for what has been given, receive the care of others and seek guidance from the Holy Spirit.

To help us along, Christianity (with its stories, teachings, prayers and rituals) offers a kind of alchemy, a process by which the despairing heart, the anxious mind, the downcast spirit might be brought into the loving Presence and transformed. In this new place we find ourselves slowly made into the loving and creative people we have longed to be.

From Jesus' perspective our sufferings provide an opportunity for awareness, insight and enlightenment. In the

Beatitudes we hear Jesus claim that our disrupted plans, our broken faith, our poverty and sufferings, our grief and unmet longings can be held as gifts that make us more compassionate toward others and more open and available to God's love.

Looking back on nearly five decades of life, it is still sometimes difficult for me to admit that my struggles, disappointments, doubts and failures in life and ministry have opened me to the very love, acceptance and peace that all my controlling behaviors sought to attain. Ultimately, grace can never be earned. Like all gifts it can only be received, requiring that I simply open my hands and trust. The more I accept difficulty as a natural part of the spiritual life, the more I find myself available to the deep gifts of the Spirit—compassion, trust, gratitude, humility, wonder, joy.

The question is how? How do we move toward trust when things fall apart? How do we receive the gifts of the Spirit when love fails us? How do we keep from sinking into despair, cynicism and apathy when injustice persists? What do we do when our faith dissipates, our friends turn to enemies, our self-worth transfigures into self-hatred? What do we do when we find ourselves enmeshed in shame, grief and judgment? How do we find God's comfort and peace when our bodies churn with frustration and anxiety?

It's interesting that Jesus had no system for helping move people from despair to hope, from fear to trust. Jesus used a number of tactics—he told stories, he confronted, he led people into nature, he put his fingers in ears and smeared mud in eyes, he stayed silent, he asked questions, he challenged preconceptions. In all that he did he sought to shift perspective. His words and actions disoriented those around him, inviting listeners to step away from their fearfulness and suffering (sometimes just for a moment), remember their humanity, and become aware of God's field of grace.

Jesus moves us to behold with compassion our suffering, the suffering of others and the suffering of the world. To do this a change of perception is required. We need some distance, some space, some practice to help us step out from our hurt and see ourselves and others through the eyes of love.

A woman is caught in adultery. She is humiliated, filled with shame. The men around her are burning with self-righteousness—and most likely, for some, fear that she might expose them as coadulterers. What does Jesus do?

He writes in the sand.

Such a strange act, so out of sync with the typical violent, shaming tension between victim and accusers. Jesus writes in the sand, and this creative act disorients. It draws people's attention away from the hurt and anger and onto this unusual teacher. When they are knocked off balance, Jesus is able to speak a word of recognition that diffuses the hostility, empowers the shamed woman and humbles the crowd, allowing everyone to become more available to God's grace. Through a change in perspective the whole unfortunate incident moves from tragedy to blessing.

We all need holding spaces where our perspective can deepen—a friend, a community, a prayer, a chapel, a story, a forest or a book to hold us until the rage calms, until the despair is comforted, until the voice of self-hatred quiets. This is what the Christian faith offers. It provides us with stories, rituals, people, imagination, sacred places and practices that move us out of confining barns with dusty oats and tepid water so we might hear and see the wider landscape of our being and receive the love of God.

We fall in holes. Plans fall apart. Dreams die. Faith disappears. Suffering is real. We need help to recalibrate our lives back to our compassionate, God-trusting selves. Often we need safe, creative space and trusted companions in order to move through hard and disorienting experiences. My hope is that the chapters in this book might provide that same creative companionship. Like life itself, this book does not present a formula for transforming difficulty into spiritual freedom (only God can bring about that mysterious conversion). What I am offering is a holding space: stories, personal experiences, honest reflections and, at the end of each chapter, practices that might help you move out of the hurt and disappointment for a moment and remember your deeper capacities for love and generosity. These same stories and practices have helped me to receive my own failings and sufferings as spiritual gifts. My ultimate hope is that you might be stirred to trust your own story as revelation, that you might begin to widen your perspective and discover that within your own struggles there awaits a (sometimes difficult and hard-won) blessing.

One caveat. There are some injustices and some losses in this life that simply feel too difficult to bear. Although there are chapters that explore grief and other deep sufferings, for the most part the chapters in this book deal with the often neglected "middle sufferings" of life—burnout, shame, vocational failure—the frustration, self-doubt and emptiness that can slowly corrupt our ability to access our deeper spiritual capacities. This book does not explore experiences in which life is not only disrupted but irreparably shattered. I do not want to suggest that all experiences can be easily held or healed, some experiences in this life can't—without time, wise and loving companions, and God's grace. My hope in those cases is that we might find a way to trust our own need for distance and safety with self-compassion, knowing that God holds the darkness we have lived through with deep sorrow and gentleness, regardless of whether we ourselves can do the same.

I often travel for work. When I return home, whether I've been away for one day or seven, whether it is late at night or early in the afternoon, whether I am confused and tired or joyful and energized, my daughter will come running. She will hear me walk across the front porch and immediately sprint for the door. As soon as she gets within four feet of me, without slowing, she will jump. She will open her arms wide and she will jump, fully trusting that I will catch her and embrace her. She does this spontaneously. I don't need to get my affairs in order. I don't need to make myself presentable. No devotional practice is needed to earn her affection. All that is required is that I come home. Disheartened or jubilant, successful or lost, whatever my state, I come home. I open the door and receive the one who loves me. And little by little my daughter's embrace brings me back to my senses, reminds me of what matters, of who matters. And when I remember, when I come home to myself, come home to God, suddenly kindness, generosity, patience and all the fruits of the Spirit become available to me.

And I can begin again.

~ 1 ~

Maddalena

The Gift of Burnout

Someone's boring me. I think it's me.

Dylan Thomas

I was stuck. Burned out. My activities both at work and home had become routine, predictable. My thought patterns looped and looped over the same tired ideas. I had been overworking, overcaring, overserving until one morning I woke up hollowed out, numb—empty of all feeling, desire, imagination. I found myself spending more and more time eating ice cream in front of the television or drinking beer on the back deck. I was tired of myself. My speaking and teaching was flat. Life had lost its mystery. God had become a chore.

"What do you need?" my wife asked me one night.

"Not to be asked questions," I told her.

For ten years I was driven. Driven to prove my worth to God and myself. Driven to attract my father's attention.

Driven to heal my childhood wounds. Driven by an ambition that often burns within young adults.

I wanted to accomplish something, to succeed. I worked hard to design and manage a new approach to spiritual formation with youth and families at our church. I developed a national research project grounded in contemplative prayer. I began coteaching spiritual formation classes at San Francisco Theological Seminary. And by working eighty to ninety hours a week, eventually I found the success I was seeking. I won grants, was featured in the *Wall Street Journal*, watched my face on ABC News, listened to my voice on national radio programs and read my words in various magazines. I was offered book contracts and speaking invitations, secured a job at the seminary, received respect and admiration from my peers as a minister and spiritual teacher. And yet inside myself I was uncaring, uninterested and lethargic. What was particularly ironic was that most of my activities involved teaching others sabbath practices of rest, silence, solitude and retreat. I was teaching and writing about what I yearned for most.

During this time my poet friend Kirk called me. We grew up together and had maintained our friendship despite living on opposite coasts. "I talked to your wife. She says you seem distant. What's going on?"

"I don't know. I guess I'm just tired."

"You sound depressed. Listen, take some time off work. I'm coming out." Two weeks later Kirk was on a plane headed west.

The night he arrived we took out maps and read guidebooks about the California coast. As we talked, it wasn't long before he noticed I was uninterested. "I actually don't care what we do."

Kirk looked at me a moment and then shrugged his shoulders, "All right, no plan. Tomorrow we drive." The next morning we loaded the car. "Let's head north, back toward the Siskiyous," Kirk said, referring to the mountains where we grew up. I had no opinion.

I drove as Kirk took out a CD. "Listen to this," he instructed. He put in the *Basement Tapes,* Bob Dylan and the Band working with classic American folk tunes. He rolled down the windows and turned up the music. "Listen to this stuff—murderers, lovers, hobos, moonshiners—they're singing about the other America. The one we don't talk about."

I listened as we drove past the dry farm fields of the Central Valley. The day was heating up. "We need beer and tacos." Kirk directed me to a stand he knew just outside of the University of California Davis, his alma mater. There were coyotes painted on the windows, and a long line of students, homeless men and suburban moms. "Go get some of that salsa," he told me. "The orange stuff." I did as I was told, found a table and sat down. Kirk returned with grilled shrimp, carnitas and a plate of corn tortillas. "I'm going to get beer. You want one?"

"I'm driving."

"So what? We'll wait it out. This is medicine."

Kirk returned and stuffed sliced limes down the golden bottlenecks. "Try the habaneras. They're hot as hell. You know that peppers release endorphins in your brain? It's the same thing as runner's high. Here, get some more of this on your shrimp, but don't touch it or you'll burn your fingers." He smiled and drank half his beer in one lift. I ate and drank mechanically, my mind empty, my mouth burning. We went out and dozed beside a patio table, our faces toward the sun. After some time, we headed north into the mountains.

Kirk lowered the window to breathe the air ripe with pine sap, forest loam and lake water. "Listen to this music!" The vocals muffled, the microphone far from Dylan's mouth, the drums heavy and slow. "You hear that tempo?" Kirk yelled to the trees, the passing cars. "It goes right to the hips. That's hip tempo, brother. Hip tempo!"

We saw signs to the Trinity Wilderness. "Turn here." Kirk pointed. We left the interstate and followed the highway along the Salmon River. The mountains were steep and soon the sun was buried by the trees, leaving the sky propane blue. We wound along the river until a yellow light bulb appeared, screwed to a wooden sign that read "Carl's Fishing Cabins." We woke the manager and paid for one night.

"Any place we can get some food?" I asked.

"Nope," the manager said, half-turned toward bed. "I can sell you a bag of pretzels."

We paid two bucks for the pretzels, and Kirk found an orange in his backpack and quartered it. We set kitchen chairs in a clearing behind the cabins and looked up at the black, moonless sky.

"I'm going to read something to you. Wait here." Kirk went indoors and came out with a nightstand. He then rummaged inside the kitchen and returned with a handful of candles, which he placed in some coffee cups and juice glasses. He lit the tilting candles, pulled a chair into their glow and opened a book. "This is Whitman. Now listen. Just feel the grief in these words."

We had no food for dinner, no plan for the next day, no television, no cell phone connection—no distraction whatsoever. So I sat outside and watched the stars spin and listened to Whitman mourn in "When Lilacs Last in the Dooryard Bloom'd":

> Sing on, sing on you gray-brown bird,
> Sing from the swamps, the recesses, pour your chant
> from the bushes,
> Limitless out of the dusk, out of the cedars and pines.
>
> Sing on dearest brother, warble your reedy song,
> Loud human song, with the voice of uttermost woe.
>
> O liquid and free and tender!
> O wild and loose to my soul—O wondrous singer!

I listened to Whitman's song, felt his grief rhythms, breathed in the forest air and quietly fell asleep.

The next morning we discovered the manager rented inflatable kayaks. We put on shorts and sunscreen, found two smashed peanut butter granola bars in the trunk for breakfast, filled water bottles, rented boats, life jackets and paddles, and had the manager shuttle us upriver.

The day was bright and the river refreshingly cool. For the morning hours we stayed quiet, each of us navigating the rapids beneath the August sun. But toward the early afternoon the river skirt spread wide and heavy, and eventually we found our kayaks gently spinning in an eddy shaded by willow trees. Our skin turning red, our bodies tired from paddling, our stomachs empty, we each lay back in our kayaks and fell asleep. It was half an hour, maybe longer, before we awoke and paddled the final half mile to the fishing cabins. We pulled our kayaks up the riverbank, returned them to the manager and headed out on the highway mad with hunger.

As we drove I remembered a restaurant where my sister had once worked. It was run by an Italian woman, Maddalena, from the island of Sardinia. The story was that Maddalena had been a celebrated five-star chef in San Francisco—but after marrying a wealthy stockbroker and weekend fisherman, she'd moved to the beautiful, tiny mountain town of Dunsmuir, located along the headwaters of the Sacramento River. Maddalena had refurbished the local train depot and turned it into a restaurant. From September through May she served dinner two nights a week, Friday and Saturday.

"That's where we're going," Kirk announced. Once we got in cell phone range I called information, and they put me through to Maddalena's.

"We have one table at 9:00 p.m."

"We'll take it," I told them.

We drove north through the winding Siskiyous and came into Dunsmuir around 7:30 p.m. We booked a room at the Super 8 Motel, found the small depot and waited outside. The building was freshly painted yellow marigold with dark crimson trim. Alongside the building was a large herb garden that smelled of oregano and rosemary. We waited, famished and dehydrated. Finally, our hour came and we took our seats.

Maddalena cooked in the middle of the room, in an open kitchen surrounded by a wooden countertop that came to just below her shoulders. She wore a white summer dress with a white apron, her black hair pulled back with a bright red bandana. She was in her midfifties, startlingly beautiful, like a middle-aged Sophia Loren—dark hair, eyes large and fierce, skin browned by the sun. She worked confidently among the fry pans and steaming pots, barking quick orders to her sous-chef. She plated the food, then slammed her hand on the counter—causing the wait staff to leave their tasks to deliver the food fresh from the fire.

We were the last to be seated, and as we perused the menu the restaurant began to empty out. The sight and smell of food made me delirious, and I found myself breaking out in lust as I read descriptions of sliced heirloom tomatoes, roasted artichoke, grilled salmon and pan-seared sea bass. We made our selections, ordered a bottle of Chianti and waited. The appetizers arrived first. Two tender half-moons of avocado filled with tiny squares of mozzarella, fresh basil leaves, cherry tomatoes, all dressed in a balsamic vinaigrette. Exquisite. Soft and rich, the food melted in our mouths. I looked at Kirk and watched his eyes fill with tears.

The waiter brought warm slices of Pugliese bread and little plates of Sicilian olives surrounded by olive oil and sea salt. We dipped the warm, crusted bread, ate the dark olives, drank our Chianti and began to laugh with a childlike pleasure at the taste of good food, the pleasure of hunger answered.

The salads arrived, crisp leaves of endive covered in ribbons of parmesan cheese. Then plates of fresh green beans, bright and sweet, pan-fired with toasted walnuts. Slowly, sacramentally, we ate the green beans—both of us now silent, reverent. The smoky walnuts, the sweet green stems—it was like eating summer itself.

Then came the main course: grilled halibut covered in toasted fennel seeds, rib-eye steak seared in peppercorns, a side dish of buttered crookneck squash and zucchini. I remember my first taste of the fish Maddalena had prepared. It was like eating love. Through tears I said to my friend, "This is communion."

The restaurant almost empty, Kirk and I, emboldened by the wine, began to cry out, "Maddalena, we worship you!" "Maddalena, you are breaking our hearts!" "Maddalena, you must come home with us!" We motherless men ate and drank and called to Maddalena, our host, our lover, our mother, the divine feminine incarnate. But Maddalena, not unaware of her powers and the effect they had on men, ignored our cries of praise. She didn't acknowledge us, nor the three or four men who lingered at her counter. Instead she stayed busy at her art, her large eyes attentive to her handiwork, her red lips even, without expression.

We ate and laughed and cried and shared our plates until Kirk pushed himself back from the table and looked at me. I returned his smile, my senses awake, my heart alive, my head full of wonder. Kirk looked at me, smiled, then called out into the half-empty room, "More wine! More wine! My friend is himself again. My friend has returned!"

I laughed, suddenly hearing the truth in his words. I had been lost, disconnected, trapped someplace within myself, outside of myself. Overworking, overthinking, overstressing, I had become stuck. But the movement of the river, the sun warm on my skin, the fasting from food, the smell of the woods, the throbbing music, the poetry of grief, the woman with ancient beauty, the culinary delights and the care of a good friend had brought me home to myself.

Without thought, I stood upon my chair and called to Maddalena. "Maddalena, you have healed me!" I raised my glass to her, and she gave me a small smile and motioned for me to sit down.

The waiter returned with our check. We were now the only patrons left in the room. "But we're still hungry," I protested. "We've traveled far, the night is young. We're not ready to leave."

"I'm sorry," he replied, "but the kitchen is closed."

"That's not possible," I protested.

"Don't you see," Kirk interrupted, "that we are two pilgrim souls? We alone can appreciate her gifts."

The young waiter looked confused and embarrassed. "Let me talk to her." We clinked our glasses and waited in full confidence that she could not turn away such devotion.

The waiter returned, "She wants to know what you want from her."

"What we want?" I shouted, my heart now burning within. "We want her to feed us. We want everything! All of it! Until we are satisfied." I stood and looked past the waiter; I looked at Maddalena standing at the center of the room. "We want everything, the whole meal, repeated. The appetizers, the bread, the salads, the vegetables, the main courses, everything, everything, everything, all over again."

At this my friend rose immediately to his feet. "Yes, yes! Exactly! Whatever the price! All of it!" We stood and watched and waited while Maddalena studied us without expression. It was nearing eleven at night, the front door was locked, the tables had been cleared and set for the next day. We waited with hope, with full hearts, with my desires returned and intact, we waited.

Then slowly, her face broke open. She looked at us, saw into our hearts, smiled and said, "Sit down."

"Hurray!" we shouted, like boys on a playground. We sat. Our table was wiped clean. Fresh napkins and silverware were placed in front of us. A new candle was lit and brought to our table, new glasses and a fresh bottle of wine set before us. We sat and we ate—slowly, gratefully, until long after midnight. We ate and laughed and cried at the flavors and talked of love, broken dreams and sorrows. We ate, and Kirk quoted poetry to Maddalena. We drank and sang songs to Maddalena. And later, as she ushered us out the front door, she kissed our cheeks goodnight. We walked across the street, collapsed in our room, and slept the deep sleep of full-hearted men.

PRACTICE

Returning to Your Senses

Reflection

- "I had been lost, disconnected, trapped someplace within myself, outside of myself. Overworking, overthinking, overstressing, I had become stuck. But the movement of the river, the sun warm on my skin, the fasting from food, the smell of the woods, the throbbing music, the poetry of grief, the woman with ancient beauty, the culinary delights and the care of a good friend had brought me home to myself." Think of a time of disconnection—a time when you felt estranged from your own passions and desires, a time when you felt distant from others. What was taking place in your life at that time? What allowed you to reconnect?

- In *Writer's Workshop in a Book* contributor Janet Finch declares that we in affluent societies have become grievously "de-natured," living lives in which the five senses have been displaced. Finch writes,

  > We know something is missing. And yet we flatter ourselves to believe that we are the advantaged souls, compared to those who walk in the out-of-doors, who cook over the smoke of a wood fire, who make their own music, who dig in the dirt, who lift and carry, who sweat in the heat of the sun, and who in the cold wrap themselves in quilts and skins. People who grow or kill their own food or shop for it in bazaars full of completely unfiltered sounds and smells and sights. We consider them disadvantaged and ourselves rich. Yet who, in this most fundamental way, is starving? I was twenty years old before I saw the moonrise for myself.

  When was the last time you felt fully (as you were as a child) awake to your senses? What are you like, what is life like, when you're aware of the sights, sounds, touch and smell of the world around you?

Action

- Christians have often needed sacred places and times to retreat from work and indulge their senses. Even Jesus regularly withdrew to mountains, the sea and other deserted places in order to be in the midst of creation, in the presence of beauty. Give yourself permission to go someplace beautiful and let yourself pray through your senses. Sit somewhere outside and focus on the smell of the trees, the grass, the earth. Find a place in the sun or sit before a real fire or pour yourself a hot bath and feel the warmth on your skin. Allow the sunlight, firelight or warm water to be a symbol of love. Spend an afternoon cooking a particularly delicious meal and experience the preparation and eating as a gift from God. Without words or reflections, allow yourself to be loved. Notice what you are like when you allow yourself to enjoy your senses.
- My burnout was a cry for help. Think of a recent time when you felt apathetic, depressed, disconnected? How was this a cry for help? If you could be a friend to your disconnected self, what would you do, what might you say? What activity might you prescribe for yourself? Write a letter to your disconnected self as if that person were a distant friend who needed a word of comfort. Set the letter aside and then, after some time, read it to yourself.

2

Prayer Service Disaster

The Gift of Disappointment

We can do no great things, only small things with great love.

Mother Teresa

The advertisement in our church newsletter was simple and straightforward: "We need someone to direct the college prayer service." I'd spent two years as a parishioner of the 250-member church and was looking for a way to serve. As a veteran youth worker, a retreat leader, an author of four books on prayer and ministry, I felt like the ad was directed at me. I met with the pastor, and she informed me the church had received a grant to develop a service that would attract students from Southern Oregon University, a school with over five thousand students, conveniently located just across the street. I told the pastor about my experience in developing prayer services for youth and adults. I showed her my books and told her about the research I'd done in spiritual formation, prayer and ministry. She was impressed and gave me the volunteer position. I was ecstatic.

Over the next month I bought hundreds of candles, built and painted a six-foot cross, collected baskets of river stones, and designed and printed song sheets. I recruited and trained a trio of local musicians (violin, piano and guitar) in various contemplative chants from Taizé, Iona and other contemplative communities. I found three elderly church members to prepare a simple supper to serve students after the service. I designed a logo, gave the service a religiously ambiguous title ("Thirst") and put ads in the college newspaper. I then met with the college chaplain and various faculty members and asked them to help spread the word about the new service. Finally, I met with student groups, mailed letters to students who had identified themselves as interested in Christianity and ate lunch each day on campus. In all my publicity I emphasized the service would provide free dinner and comfort for stressed-out students.

The night before the service I couldn't sleep. I had visions of undergraduates, weary and lost, showing up to the service. I thought about the conversations I would initiate once the service ended. I began to dream about a campus Bible study or maybe a theological reflection group. I imagined taking a core group of students on a service trip to Mexico during the spring recess. The possibilities were endless. I was excited to see what God would do.

I showed up three hours before our first service. I helped prepare soup and then set up the chapel. I removed the front pews, placed the large wooden cross on the floor, filled metal trays with sand and primitive clay bowls with water and floating candles, set out fresh flowers, and placed warm-colored icons at the perimeter. I then sat in the chapel and prayed. I'd been praying for the service all along, but tonight I wanted extra time to pray. I sat by the cross, lit a candle, and in silence I asked God to bless the service. I prayed for the students, prayed that all my work would bear fruit in the lives of the students. My heart filled with a quiet joy as I sat in the beautiful chapel, grateful for the work that God was doing, grateful that I had been called to serve such a beautiful vision.

Fifteen minutes before the service began I lit the candles around the chapel, opened the front doors of the church, picked up a handful of the service bulletins and stood at the church entrance. Immediately, I saw a group of fifteen students walk across the street from the university. I smiled with warmth and gratitude as the students stepped onto the sidewalk in front of the church. They looked at me, a young woman waved, and then they turned and walked to the nearby grocery store. I stood and watched as various students passed by on the sidewalk, some glancing at me with curiosity, most oblivious to me and the beautiful prayer service. At five minutes past the designated hour, I walked inside. There were the three musicians at the back of the room, the pastor, the three elderly women who fixed the evening meal, and me. That was it. Two months of work and prayer and preparation, and not one student.

If I ever become an actor and have a scene where I need to make myself cry, it will be easy. I'll only need to think of that first college prayer service I facilitated. It was the saddest service I've ever witnessed—and I don't mean Jesus in Gethsemane praying "I am sorrowful unto death" kind of sad. I mean more like overweight middle-aged white man at an Usher concert singing "I am a sex machine" kind of sad.

Midway through the service the bulletin instructed participants to come forward and pray around the large cross that lay on the floor. There were baskets of candles so that after people knelt down, they could light a candle and place it in one of the sand trays along the edge of the cross. When the moment arrived the three elderly women stood up. All three of them were well into their seventies, but they liked me and wanted to support the service, so they walked forward. There was a long, anxious pause as the three women stopped at the foot of the cross and contemplated the distance to the floor. Finally, one woman gripped the arms of her two companions and carefully lowered her buttocks until she reached a half-squat. She paused for a few seconds, then like a deep-sea diver, suddenly released her hands and fell back with a hard thump onto the carpeted floor. "My goodness!" she cried out. *God help us!* I thought to myself.

The second woman walked to the left side of the wooden cross, stretched her arms out and bent at the waist with her knees locked. She tilted forward like a windblown tree until her hands struck the floor. Now in an upside down *V*, her backside raised to the heavens, the woman stretched out her legs and began to walk her fingers forward until her arms suddenly gave out and she collapsed face down on the floor. Alarmed, the third woman hurried to help her prostrate friend, but she tripped on the candle basket and crumpled over on top of her. All of this took place while the pastor, the three musicians and I chanted, "Stay with me, remain here with me, watch and pray. Watch and pray."

For the next nine months I led the weekly college prayer service. Not one college student ever attended. Not one. I spent hundreds of hours visiting the campus, tacking up flyers, placing ads in the college paper, meeting student groups, but not one student ever walked across the street—not even for the free postservice dinner (which we eventually stopped serving).

My life has never matched my expectations. Never. Sometimes life exceeds my expectations, other times it falls short; more often life does something unusual, unexpected, unpredictable, something that renders my expectations absurd. I often find myself living within a world of expectations—the expectations of family, pastors, neighbors and the surrounding culture. The most damning expectations, however, come from deep within, goading me, judging me, criticizing me for falling short.

Expectations in ministry and life often arise from two distracting energies: worry and fantasy. Anxious expectations are grounded in the fear of failure. They are nurtured by the belief that our accomplishments determine our value and worth. This is the message in our secular culture, and this is frequently the driving force within most Christians. Some voice inside of us tells us that faithful people are successful. Deep down we believe if we pray, follow the Ten Commandments and work hard, God will grant us a successful life. When our lives fail to match our expectations, we get anxious, work harder, worry more and eventually God moves to the margin of our lives.

Expectations are also built out of fantasy. The spiritual life is hard. There are few tangible rewards. It's much more pleasurable to dream of social justice, to talk of serving the poor, than to actually do it. In Dostoevsky's *The Brothers Karamazov*, an elderly monk, a wise man named Father Zossima, converses with a wealthy woman. The woman is in anguish about the existence of God. The wise elder tells her only by acts of love will she be able to know God. "Try to love your neighbors, love them actively and unceasingly. And as you learn to love them more and more, you will be more and more convinced of the existence of God and of the immortality of your own soul."

At first Zossima's words comfort the woman. She confesses she often imagines giving away her wealth in order to live a life of poverty and service to the poor. She tells the father that this image often brings her tears of joy. But then, as she entertains the fantasy of a life of Christian service, she worries the people she would serve would be unappreciative of her sacrifice and efforts. She realizes she would be unable to tolerate ingratitude. "I want to be praised and paid for love with love." And so her dream of serving others dies and she continues to wonder if God exists.

How do we live with the great disappointment of Christian living? How do we continue to serve when our lives don't match our expectations? What do we do when our efforts, our commitment to Jesus, our prayers and spiritual yearnings don't pay off? During the nine months that I directed the college prayer service, I began to read the

Gospels—paying special attention to the disciples' experience. I began to feel the confusion, helplessness, frustration, anxiety, fear and even ambivalence the disciples often experienced. For the disciples Jesus was often a bewildering disappointment. He acted in ways that seemed completely unproductive compared to the disciples' expectations. In the final interaction between Jesus and his followers (Acts 1) you can sense their disappointment. Still expecting Jesus to overthrow the Roman oppressors, the disciples ask, "Is this the time when you will restore the kingdom to Israel?" Jesus responds, "It is not for you to know." He ascends, and the disciples depart, still unclear of what the future will bring.

Again and again the disciples are forced to give up their control and expectations, and remain in a state of spiritual poverty. To enter into spiritual poverty is to keep from seeking to possess or control God. Spiritual poverty is the willingness to be empty, to allow our expectations of God to dissipate. Like those who followed Jesus, it's a willingness to be helpless, confused, anxious and wanting. It's a willingness to enter the void, the uncertainty that so many people, particularly the poor, live with every day. It's a willingness to allow God to be God and me to be me. It's only in this empty and vulnerable state that we become available to the God who lives in the present moment, the God who lives in our immediate relationships and the God who lives within the small acts of love that we are asked to undertake.

Over nine months the college prayer service grew to about thirty souls—still mostly women over sixty years old. In the spring, one month before the service was going to break for the summer, I met with the pastor and resigned my position. I felt like a failure. One month later Kim, the pianist from the prayer service I had hired from a music school, asked to meet with me. When we met she told me her story. It was a heartbreaking history of abuse, betrayal, grief and sorrow. When she finished she told me, "I don't know anything about religion. I don't know anything about God, but I heard you were quitting the prayer service and I wanted to thank you for what you've done because it is the only thing I've looked forward to each week. I want to become a Christian, even though I don't know what that means. And I wanted to ask if you would be my sponsor."

Three years later the "college prayer service" continues. Every Tuesday night somewhere between fifteen and thirty people gather to sing and pray, sit in silence and listen to Scripture. The heavy wooden cross has been replaced with a table cross so that the elderly folks can light candles without kneeling on the floor. In the back of the room sit the same three musicians I hired three years ago. The violinist frequents our church retreats and youth programs; the guitarist, having suffered a painful divorce, often comes to a weekly Christian meditation group; and Kim the pianist now leads the Sunday morning music.

We minister because we want to know love; we want to live love. To live a life of love is to trust what we're given more than what we give. The Christian path is a commitment to practicing the art of love, learning the dimensions and character of love—its boundless depth, its endless horizon. On the Christian path we are learning to let go of our expectations—the expectations of ourselves, of God, of others. We are learning to live in spiritual poverty, to be empty, open, helpless, uncertain, so we might be available to God's hidden, humble work.

When the wealthy woman in *The Brothers Karamazov* admits she can't serve God if her service will be unappreciated, Father Zossima responds,

> A true act of love, unlike imaginary love, is hard and forbidding. . . . [It] requires hard work and patience, and for some, it is a whole way of life. But I predict that at the very moment when you see despairingly that, despite all your efforts, you have not only failed to come closer to your goal but, indeed, seem even farther from it than ever—at that very moment, you will have achieved your goal and will recognize the miraculous power of our Lord, who has always loved you and has secretly guided you all along.

PRACTICE

Remembering Gratitude

Reflection

- "My life has never matched my expectations." What are the expectations that you have carried for your life or ministry? See if you might recall the expectations you had for your life when you were young—a teenager or young adult. What kind of family did you expect to have in adulthood? What were your expectations for career?

What kind of person did you expect you would become? Make a list of these expectations (if it's helpful, use the categories of family, career, self, spiritual life).

- After you complete the list, go through the items and ask yourself where these expectations came from (culture, family, personal need, joy, hope). As you reflect on each of these expectations do you see them as gift or burden? Have these expectations brought you life, joy, generosity, love and other fruits of the Spirit, or have they made you more anxious, frustrated, bitter and disappointed with yourself and others? After reflecting on each of these, read this word from Jesus as if spoken to you from a compassionate friend: "Do not be anxious about your life, what you will eat, nor about your body, what you will put on. For life is more than food, and the body more than clothing. Consider the ravens: they neither sow nor reap, they have neither storehouse nor barn, and yet God feeds them. Of how much more value are you than the birds!" (Luke 12:22-24 ESV).
- In what way has Christianity (or God) disappointed you? At times you can sense Jesus' friends and followers feel disappointed. What do you sense Jesus would say to you about your disappointment? How might your disappointment invite you to see God, yourself and others more honestly?
- In what ways are you spiritually poor? Take a moment to be honest and behold the reality of this poverty in your life. Jesus says, "Blessed are the poor in spirit" (Matthew 5:3). In what way has your spiritual poverty been a gift, to you or to others?

Action

- Our minds often perseverate on failure, mistakes and our shortcomings. This focus on what's missing narrows our perspective, blinding us to the actual gifts and graces that come to us. Ignatius of Loyola, the founder of the Jesuits, taught his community a prayer called "the Awareness Examen," which invites us to look over our experience, seeking to notice moments of grace. Find a quiet place where you can pray undisturbed. Take a few moments to relax and rest, gently becoming aware of God's presence, or the presence of Jesus, within and around you.
- When you are ready, invite God or Jesus to accompany you as you look over the previous day or maybe as you look over a recent ministry activity. As you remember and recall all the activities of the day (or go through all the experiences of a particular ministry event), allow this question to arise: For what moment was I most grateful? Allow little things to emerge: a smile from a stranger, the sunlight through a window, a hug from your daughter, an engaging conversation. Choose one of these moments to meditate on. Don't force anything—just be open and let the moment arise that seems to hold the most gratitude. Then let yourself relive the experience, recalling what you saw, felt and heard in that encounter.
- What is being offered to you in this moment? What does this moment tell you about yourself, about your life with God? What is it like to sit in gratitude? Take a few moments to journal any thoughts, prayers, reflections.

What does your disappointment, your sense of spiritual poverty, look like when you put it in relationship with the gratitude that you are now aware of?

3

Idiots

The Gift of Difficult People

The love of our neighbor in all
its fullness simply means being able to
say, "What are you going through?"

Simone Weil

Henry Ward Beecher once wrote, "God sends ten thousand truths, which come about us like birds seeking inlet; but we are shut up to them, and so they bring us nothing, but sit and sing awhile upon the roof, and then fly away." The tragedy in life is not necessarily the suffering that life brings but the way we ignore, defend against and shut ourselves off from the ten thousand truths, the ten thousand beauties that seek to heal, awaken and free us to the life we long to live.

Each encounter with another human being carries the possibility of changing how we experience the world. In each encounter with another soul we can be struck by beauty, changed by the heartbreak of another person's struggle, or we can become hardened, wounded, drawn into judgment and criticism, unable to apprehend that despite how they present themselves, the person in front of us embodies one of God's ten thousand faces.

I gathered with a group of friends at our favorite pub to listen to David talk about his experience at a weeklong contemplative retreat. "The silence was healing. The prayer was rich and meaningful. The spiritual directors were wise and caring. There was only one problem."

"What was that?"

"The idiots." We looked confused.

"Two idiots to be exact. Married idiots. Every time we were led in a guided meditation, this woman would start dancing in the middle of the circle, in front of everyone, with this big smile on her face. It was so damn distracting. And then we'd be sitting in silent prayer and her husband would start making these little chuckles and 'Mmms' as if he was having this really intimate conversation with God. Sometimes I had to leave the room in the middle of prayer because I could feel I was going to choke the guy and start yelling, 'Okay Chuckles, let's hear you laugh *now*!'"

We spent the rest of the evening complaining about various annoying people we'd encountered in church and ministry, each of us telling stories of difficult people who'd driven us nuts. One friend who had recently quit the ministry confessed, "I couldn't stand the people. I loved worship. I love God. It was the people I couldn't stand. Why are there so many annoying people in church? It's like a gathering place for all those needy for attention. I couldn't take it."

We nodded our heads knowingly when Jeremy offered, "But aren't there also saints?" We looked at each other—lips greased from burgers, cheeks reddened by Oregon ale and the late hour. No one responded. We were pastors, youth workers, teachers—professional Christians—yet the poverty of our own lives was obvious. Certainly none of us were holy. The truth was we more closely resembled the very idiots we had been complaining about all evening. We gazed awkwardly at the table. Then Laura saved us.

"I met a man. A Franciscan. It was a one-day conference on nonviolence. I was up in the front pew. Next to me was this pretentious woman who sat with her spine straight, legs crossed in some yoga contortion. She had this very serene look on her face. Too serene. She held some kind of prayer beads, and when she saw me, she gave me this little bow and smiled with this sweet, peaceful smile—the kind that makes you want to empty your bowels in public.

"The two presenters were former military men, and just before the conference began, these two guys were razzing each other. One was ex-Navy, the other Army. They were making jokes—Army versus Navy jokes. One would say, 'Can you hand me those notebooks?' And the other would say, 'You Navy guys, always expect someone else to do your bidding.' They'd laugh, and then the Navy guy would make some equally cutting comment.

"It was clear these guys were friends, but the woman next to me was getting visually agitated. She'd frown at the men, then close her eyes and exhale loudly. She was trying to do everything you expect a holy person to do—you know, act peaceful, serene and unfazed by it all. The two presenters called everyone to attention and began the workshop when the woman next to me raised her hand.

"She stood and confronted the presenters. She told them she overheard their conversation and was so disturbed and appalled by the way they joked about the military that she was considering leaving the conference. She started lecturing the presenters in a loud voice so that the whole room wouldn't miss a word—'Don't you understand the violence the US military is engaged in!'

"She went on and on while these two poor guys just stood there looking awkward and embarrassed—two guys, by the way, who'd seen military combat, two committed Christians who'd spent many months in prison for nonviolent protests against US involvement in Iraq. And yet this woman, heavily made up and sporting an expensive-looking yoga outfit, lectured them about what's appropriate.

"She finished her tirade, and the whole audience was just seething at this woman. She was so full of herself, so pompous. She made a big deal of packing up her things, like she was too holy to be involved in the workshop. All of us couldn't wait for her to go.

"Then, all of sudden, from somewhere in the back of the room this elderly man started walking forward. He had this look of anguish on his face.

"He knelt down next to this woman and with a pained look said he could see that she had been hurt. He took her hand and told her how sorry he was that this occurred. He told her that these presenters were actually good men, and that whatever pain they'd caused was unintentional. He then asked her to stay for the conference.

"All of us were in shock. This woman was so false and self-important, just like the people we've been talking about, and yet this man took her seriously, offering her respect and dignity—more dignity than she offered the presenters, more dignity than we offered her.

"The rest of the day we talked about the nonviolence of Jesus and did all sorts of analysis and went through a bunch of exercises. But the thing that will stick with me most was the presence of this man—his compassion for someone who was so pretentious and annoying."

"What was his name?" I asked.

"Father Louis Vitale," was her response.

I went home that night and Googled Louis Vitale. I found out he's a Franciscan monk and a primary leader of the nuclear-freeze movement of the 1980s. He spent years in jail for protesting nuclear testing in Nevada. He was also head of the Franciscans in North America but got in trouble when he tried to give away the order's endowment to the poor.

I read that he spent the past ten years working with homeless folks in San Francisco. He let them sleep and eat in St. Basil's Cathedral at all hours, even when church and city leaders protested. I read and read and then found out that, sure enough, he was currently in a federal penitentiary in El Centro, California.

In November of 2006 he and Jesuit Stephen Kelly had attempted to deliver a letter opposing the teaching of torture techniques at Fort Huachuca, Arizona—headquarters of US Army Intelligence and the training center for military interrogators. The priests were arrested as they knelt in prayer halfway up the driveway at the army base.

I checked my travel schedule and saw that I had an upcoming event in San Diego. On a whim, I sent an email to Father Vitale's community, asking if I could visit Vitale at the jail. The next day I received a reply. He was only allowed two visitors a week, and visits could only last thirty minutes. The community was willing to give me a slot. I extended my trip and reserved a rental car. A month later my friend Frank and I made the drive two hours east of San Diego to El Centro.

"Why are we doing this again?" my friend asked as we crossed the dry desert.

"Laura said he's a holy man," I replied. "Don't you want to meet a holy man?"

In the Imperial County Jail, behind a two-inch-thick Plexiglas wall stood seventy-six-year-old Father Louis Vitale in an orange jumpsuit. He had a large, slightly goofy grin. His white, half-moon hair stuck up like he'd rubbed it with a balloon. After the guards unlocked his shackles, Father Vitale waved at Frank and me, then sat down while lifting two heavy black phones to each ear—one for Frank and one for me.

"Welcome to the Imperial Jail!" he shouted.

The first thing I noticed was how excited he was to talk to people. He spoke rapidly, almost hyperactively, moving from topic to topic. It was as if we were continuing some conversation that had to be completed in haste.

He told us about the facility—no windows, fluorescent lights glaring twenty-four hours a day. Meals were served at odd, irregular times—breakfast between three and four in the morning, for instance. He talked about the inmates—mostly Mexicans arrested for crossing the border. He told us he was learning Spanish so he could communicate with his cellmate.

He talked about being in solitary confinement for the first months of his one-year imprisonment. He said he enjoyed it. It was like his novitiate (the time period before taking priestly vows)—lots of solitude and silence, time to pray. He told us Martin Luther King Jr. once said that in a cell, alone, in silence, is where real prayer can happen. He told us he found that to be true.

He told us of the letters he received, "All these people who tell me they're praying for me. I just feel so loved. If everyone could receive letters like I'm getting here in prison, the world would be a better place."

He talked about his years in the air force and his epiphany that the military consisted of regular people who meant well but made mistakes. On and on he talked without giving us any space to reply. I began wondering if this guy was holy or just crazy. He reminded me of homeless men I'd met on the streets of our town—men who seem half-crazed, act overly familiar and speak in meandering streams of consciousness.

I thought a man of compassion would be calm, serene, self-contained. Father Vitale was the opposite—excited, energized, talkative, eager to connect. He laughed often, and he looked us in the eyes with something like an intense friendliness.

I interrupted with a question: "Why are you in jail?"

He paused. His face changed demeanor. A kind of grief came over him as he said, "Hearing that this country is engaging in torture just hit me in the gut. It should hit everyone in the gut. That's where I feel God: in my gut. I just had to do something. I think if I didn't I'd just get depressed."

He leaned forward toward the glass and paused to look me in the eye. "This isn't just about the victims," he added. "This is about the people who have to inflict the suffering as well." He told me about Alyssa Peterson, a young US Army interpreter who trained at Ft. Huachuca. She was sent as part of the interrogation team to one of the US prisons in Iraq. After just two sessions in the cages, she died by suicide.

We talked about America's involvement in Iraq. He rattled off the history of US involvement in Abu Ghraib prison and the creation of Guantanamo Bay. But what was most striking in this conversation was Father Vitale's demeanor toward people. Torture is a serious issue, and obviously Vitale has been responding with his life—yet his demeanor was light. He smiled and laughed easily; there was little animosity in his voice toward the military or government leaders and officials who authorized and advocated torture.

This was different than most activists, even Christian activists I'd met. Many of them seemed angry, repressing the same kind of violence they sought to counter. In conversing with Father Vitale, I noticed how often he tried to see things through the perspective of the other, the military, the policemen who arrested him, the presidential administration.

"I can see myself in their shoes," he said. "I used to be in the military; I shared many of their viewpoints at one time." When I asked him how he's able to avoid bitterness and anger and demonizing those who've placed him in prison, he smiled and said, "Well, I like people. I've always liked people. I've never met anyone who I wanted dead. I've never met a person who I wanted to suffer in hell or anything like that. I've always liked people."

Then he told us about a man who was recently brought into the prison. He had murdered his stepfather in a particularly cruel and inhuman manner. Vitale nodded over to the visitor booth next to us. We saw a middle-aged Caucasian man with a shaved head—his arms, hands, and neck covered in tattoos. "That's the guy there," Vitale told us. "All the inmates want to kill him. He shouts and screams all night long so no one can sleep. He shouts the most awful obscenities at the guards. He throws urine and feces at people through his cell bars. I think he probably has some kind of mental illness."

Vitale paused, then continued. "If I stand on my bed, I can just see into the top of his cell. I can see his television set. The other night, about two in the morning, it was quiet. I couldn't sleep. I stood on my bed and looked over and could see that this guy had his television on. I could just see the top of his head. He was standing watching a documentary on the Egyptian pyramids."

Vitale paused again and smiled. "Now, you just gotta have a soft spot for a guy like that."

The guards tapped him on the shoulder. He stood, and they handcuffed him behind his back.

Vitale smiled at us again—a big goofy grin—and then yelled. Loud enough so we could hear him through the glass.

"Don't feel sorry for me! I'm a blessed man!"

I walked out of the jail and immediately started laughing. What a nut! He was nothing like I'd expected. He didn't match any of my images of holiness. On my drive back to San Diego I tried to process what holiness might mean in relation to others and how Vitale was nudging me to see that the annoying, the difficult and even the dangerous people I encounter provide an opportunity to grow in love for myself and others.

What struck me was Vitale's deep acceptance of himself. There was no persona. He confessed his faults and gifts without shame or false modesty. The essence of his religious commitment was in his struggle to feel connected to each person he encountered—even those who were threatening or repulsive. Vitale's practice was to search (with a kind of playful curiosity) for the humanity, the divine spark in each person he met. In my interview with Vitale I watched again and again as he struggled to find something likeable in people, some kind of connection that he could feel in his gut that would release a real sense of understanding and empathy for victims as well as perpetrators.

This was, in a sense, the essence of Vitale's spiritual genius. For Vitale, difficult people stimulated his curiosity. The more different or difficult the person, the more curious Vitale became: Why does this person act this way? What might they have suffered that would cause this behavior? Where is the divine spark in this person? How does this person come to life? What's beautiful about this person?

When Jesus asks us to pray for our enemies he is inviting this very same curiosity, understanding and empathy.

Rather than feeling annoyed or bitter or angry toward people, Vitale receives people as a blessing, an opportunity to encounter God, to make contact with his own brokenness, an occasion to share the compassion of Jesus. Maybe this blessing comes from receiving others as potential emissaries from God. Maybe it comes from a deep awareness of one's own faults. Maybe it means learning to approach those people who are difficult for us as opportunities to deepen our compassion for ourselves and others, and to enjoy the wild diversity of God's love.

A few months after my friend had complained about "the idiots" at his retreat, I was visiting a colleague who had served as a spiritual director at the same retreat. We were talking about suffering when he told me, "You know I was on staff at this contemplative retreat that your friend attended. There was this couple who had traveled from the Midwest. They had lost their son the previous year and needed a retreat to try to deal with their grief. We had these times for silent meditations, and each time the father would start chuckling. One time I asked him, 'I notice you often laugh during the silent prayer. May I ask why?' The guy turns to me with tears in his eyes and says, 'In the silence I close my eyes and see my son and remember times when we laughed together, and then I start laughing and it helps me feel that somehow he's okay.'"

Who could have known that a behavior so irritating and annoying contained such grief and tenderness? Again, I felt the power of Vitale's genius, to approach others with curiosity (particularly those whose behavior is difficult to abide), to work to place myself within the experience of others (even if this means imagining what experiences might be behind their behavior), and then to wait until the divine spark that burns in every heart becomes visible. To wait until my own compassion rises to the surface so that my actions (whether confrontational or empathic) are grounded in love.

PRACTICE

Beholding a Difficult Person

Reflection

- Each encounter with another human being carries the possibility of changing how we experience the world. In a flash we can be struck by the beauty, the struggle or the suffering of one of Christ's ten thousand faces. Think of someone in your life who you would describe as beautiful. The author refers to Father Vitale as a saint. In your experience, what are the qualities of a holy person? How has suffering made Father Vitale more loving?
- Who in your life do you find repulsive? What is it about this person that causes this reaction in you? Imagine for a moment the experiences this person may have gone through in childhood that would cause him or her to be the person he or she has become. See if you can understand why this person behaves this way. Can you feel compassion for a child who has undergone the kind of experiences that you imagine this person encountered?

- Although Vitale says he understands and carries no hatred toward US government officials who advocate for and perpetrate torture on others, he is still seeking to confront and combat their behavior. He does this, he says, because he feels the wrongness of torture "in his gut." There is something right about Vitale's gut reaction that seeks peace, human dignity and an end to suffering. Reflect on the repulsion, anger or frustration that you experience toward a specific person. What is appropriate about this reaction in you? What is the good desire within this reaction? How might you respond to this reaction in a way that is appropriate and life giving?

Action

- My wife believes that there would be more kindness in the world if everyone pinned their baby picture to the front of their shirt. It would be difficult to disregard or demonize others if you had an image that reminded you of their humanity—reminded you of their soft, innocent beginning.
- Find a place and time where you can sit in quiet reflection. After a few moments, bring to mind a person in your life who repulses, irritates or angers you. Using your imagination, picture this person as if he or she were a small child. What do you think this person's hopes were when he or she was little? What fears do you imagine this person carried as a child? What experiences can you imagine the person experienced that shaped him or her into the person he or she is today? Take a few minutes to simply gaze on this person without judgment.

It might help you to write down what you notice. After you finish this reflection, see if there is a new invitation for how you might interact with this person based on what you've experienced in your reflection.

4

Graduation Day

The Gift of Brokenness

I must unapologetically reveal my broken life as a thing of beauty.

Cornel West

Into the world we come as soft and fragile as the most delicate of orchids. We come in need of care, of love. We come in need of welcoming eyes and listening ears. We come with hearts trusting that we will be received and celebrated, we come ready to receive and celebrate others. The betrayal that many of us experience as children is devastating. Never do we open and trust as completely as when we were children. The protective barriers that we build up are so difficult to dismantle. Often they are never dismantled, only accepted as a part of who we are.

But once in a while, in graced moments, in solitude, in friendship, in prayer, in surprising moments of self-discovery, in creative acts of love, the ramparts come down, the walls melt, the hidden past suddenly releases, and we find something that only a child's heart could hope for and dream possible.

My wife met a woman named Teresa. Teresa had been raised in a household with two alcoholic parents who were often lost in a neglectful fog. Teresa was forced to raise herself. As young as three years old, she remembers searching for food, hungrily rummaging through cupboards and vacant refrigerators, eating dry cereal while her parents lay passed out on the floor.

In the few childhood photographs that exist, Teresa wears unwashed and ill-fitting clothes. In school photos her hair is matted and unkempt, her face is unsmiling, heavy with worry. If you were to only see her childhood photos you would assume she was an orphan, a refugee, a girl living in a cardboard box. You would never guess that Teresa was raised in a nice house, with two parents, in a middle-class suburb. Teresa was an afterthought, a side note, a child ignored by two parents absorbed in addiction. Unsocialized, nervous and hurting, Teresa grew up quiet and withdrawn. She remembers few social interactions, no neighborhood friends, no school activities. She lived shrouded in loneliness.

In fifth grade, however, Teresa discovered something about herself. She was smart. She was good at reading. Mathematics came naturally. She easily grasped the lessons her teacher taught and found her mind hungry for ideas. Her teacher noticed Teresa's intelligence and provided her with a steady supply of books. Her mind awake, Teresa spent hours tucked away in the public library trying to forget her parents, her pain. As her mind expanded, a new sense of self-worth began to grow. Despite her parents' lack of involvement and her own emotional isolation, Teresa poured herself into school work. In middle school she had straight As. In high school, she was placed in all the advanced classes and soon was one of the top students in her school.

Teresa looked forward to high school graduation being a high point of her life. She looked forward to being one of only a handful of students who would wear a gold cord over the black graduation robe as a sign of academic achievement. She looked forward to receiving this recognition in front of her classmates and the larger community. When the graduation ceremony took place, Teresa sat on stage in the high school auditorium feeling a rare and deep sense of pride. With the gold cord over her robe, her gifts were finally visible. Her classmates and the larger community could now see that she was bright, that she was intelligent, that she had value and worth.

The graduates were seated, the speeches were given and finally the principal stood to present the diplomas. Before making the presentation, however, he made this fateful announcement: "In order to expedite the ceremony, I would like to ask that the audience postpone all applause until all the graduates have received their diplomas. In order to save time, we need everyone to please remain silent when a graduate's name is called. Once all the students have their diplomas, we will applaud them together."

The problem with this instruction was that no one obeyed. Despite numerous reminders to remain quiet, each time a name was announced clusters of relatives, friends and classmates would stand and cheer—even when reprimanded by the principle. Soon Teresa noticed that every graduate had received applause and a sick feeling began to well up inside of her, *What if when my name is read, the room remains silent?*

Friendless, Teresa knew she had no hope of receiving any sounds of approval from her classmates. She anxiously began to scan the audience for her parents. Finally, she located her father standing with a drinking buddy against the back wall. She could tell by his slack shoulders he was drunk. Her mother was nowhere to be seen. She narrowed her eyes and stared at her father, willing him to notice her, to notice her predicament, praying that he and his friend would make some kind of commotion when her name was read.

Finally, her name was called. Her father remained stoic, either indifferent or unaware that his daughter was receiving a diploma. Teresa waited a beat hoping for some kind of noise, some kind of recognition. There was none. She stood, made her way through the row of seated graduates and walked across the stage in silence. After receiving her diploma, she walked back to her seat and felt herself burning with shame at the echoes of her dress shoes clacking across the walls of the auditorium. When the ceremony ended, she quietly placed her diploma, her robe and her honor cord in a trash can near the exit and walked home in tears. She had been the only graduate greeted by silence.

Teresa cut herself off from her parents and worked her way through a reputable college three thousand miles from her hometown. Still withdrawn, still emotionally and socially isolated, Teresa spent all her time either working or studying. Although her grades placed her at the top of her class, she skipped her college graduation ceremony, still wounded by her experience in high school. She went on to law school. Again she filled her life with work and study; she passed the bar and earned her degree with honors.

At the encouragement of one of her professors she decided to attend the law school graduation. On the morning of the ceremony she arrived wearing her robe and honor cord. As she arrived at the site she suddenly had a flashback of the shame she experienced at her high school graduation ceremony. Anxious to prevent another scene of humiliation, Teresa found a small group of teenagers just beyond the seated audience. She took out the graduation program, showed them her name and then paid them to cheer for her when her name was announced. The teenagers were somewhat mystified by the request, but they took the money and promised to applaud when her name was called.

Teresa took her seat, and sure enough, just as she feared, when it came time to award the diplomas, the dean asked that the audience hold their applause until all the graduates had received their diplomas. Once again, just as she had feared, each graduate had a smattering of friends and family that cheered despite the dean's instructions. When Teresa's name was read, she stood, hoping that at least the teenagers, whom she had paid, would applaud. Unfortunately, they were distracted and missed their cue. She stood, and for the second time in her life she walked across a public stage in silence.

That night all the shame, all the hurt, all the loneliness of her life overwhelmed her. She had worked so hard to prove her worth, to keep herself distracted from her own grief and sadness. The graduation ceremony had exposed her, exposed her loneliness, her isolation, her failure to garner love and admiration.

That night Teresa began to drink. Over the next six years Teresa's addiction led her to live on the streets of San Francisco as an alcoholic. She lived in cars and homeless shelters, she slept with men for drinks, for food, for shelter from the cold. Finally, one morning, after nearly dying of exposure, Teresa stumbled across a twelve-step group. She eventually stopped drinking, got a job as a legal secretary for a small nonprofit, rented a studio apartment and after a few years met Johann—a cheerful, stable man in her apartment complex. After a brief courtship they married.

Two years later, on the night of her thirty-fifth birthday, she returned home from work to a surprise party. The lights flicked on and suddenly there were streamers, balloons and congratulatory signs. Neighbors, workmates and members from Teresa's twelve-step group were all dressed up and cheering. Teresa was completely shocked—she had never had a birthday party before. To make up for all the lost birthdays, her husband included children's party hats, a bright children's birthday cake, childhood games like pin the tale on the donkey and a scavenger hunt with candy prizes. There were childlike gifts in bright wrapping paper—coloring sets, bouncy balls, dress-up dolls and other gifts Teresa should have experienced as a youngster. The laughter, the care, the playfulness, the games—all awakened a deep sense of healing in Teresa.

After all the gifts had been opened, Johann gathered everyone around the television set. After a few introductory comments, he placed a DVD into the player and onto the screen came a celebration of Teresa's life. There were photographs and music, interviews with many of Teresa's new friends, quotes about all the beautiful traits that Teresa possessed.

Then suddenly, at the end of the montage, appeared the faded video of a graduation ceremony—the very same law school graduation ceremony that Teresa had attended a decade earlier. The school dean and other administrators were standing at the podium handing out the diplomas to the waiting graduates. Shocked, Teresa sat and watched as the dean read her name. She watched as this young, driven, hurting woman stood to receive her diploma. She watched as her younger self walked across the stage and then braced herself for the traumatizing silence. But the silence never came. Instead, remarkably, she began to hear a rolling cascade of applause, cheers and then her husband's voice hooting and hollering and calling out across the auditorium, "Way to go, Teresa!" and "You did it, Teresa!"

Three months prior Johann had contacted the law school and purchased a copy of Teresa's graduation ceremony. Johann worked as a recording engineer, and after he received the tape, he set up his equipment in a local auditorium. He recorded his voice over one hundred times as he sat in different locations, cheered in high- and low-pitch voices, whooped and hollered, and called out his wife's name. He then edited all of these voices together onto one track and dubbed this new recording onto the graduation tape—so that this time, as Teresa walked across the stage, she was greeted with wild approval.

Teresa watched in bewildered amazement as her younger self received her diploma to the sound of cheers and applause. Then suddenly, before she knew what was happening, something erupted within her. She stood up, pointed at the screen and heard herself shout, "Turn it off! That's not how it happened! " She turned and ran into the bedroom, slammed the door and collapsed onto the bed wailing and crying.

Gently, repentantly, her husband entered the bedroom and tried to apologize. She screamed at him to leave her alone, "You knew how painful that was to me. How dare you put that up on a screen! How dare you try to cover it up!" Awkward and distraught, Johann asked the guests to leave. He took down the streamers and balloons, cleaned up the cake and drinks, and stashed the toys and gifts into the closet while Teresa lay weeping. Then he took a sleeping bag and made a bed in the study.

It was almost three in the morning when Teresa finally calmed. She had wept from wounds that cut all the way back to childhood and maybe further—into infancy, into the womb itself. She wept the unwept tears of physical abuse and neglect, shaming glances, rejection and emotional cruelty that she had suffered as a child. Now all was still. Quiet and empty.

She rose up and walked out into the living room. She opened the refrigerator and took out a piece of birthday cake. It was chocolate with vanilla icing. Her favorite. She rummaged through the closet and found the toy doll, the coloring books, the crayons and party hats. She carefully placed these objects on the coffee table and examined them while eating her cake on a party plate that said "Celebrate!" When the cake was eaten, she got up, turned on the television and placed the birthday DVD into the player.

Johann heard Teresa out in the living room. Racked with guilt, he had spent the night listening to Teresa's anguish, berating himself for the pain he had resurrected. He heard the television turn on and then slowly, apprehensively, he walked out from the study. Teresa looked at him and smiled remorsefully, with dabs of frosting at the corners of her mouth. Johann smiled back. Then, without speaking, he stood behind her and gently placed his hands on her shoulders. Teresa picked up the remote and scanned the DVD he had made, forwarding the images until she found the clip from the law school graduation. Teresa pushed the play button, turned up the sound and watched the video for a second time.

Teresa watched as her name was called. She watched as her younger self stood up. She watched as the young graduate cast her eyes down. She watched as the young woman walked with shoulders stiff and protective. Teresa watched and listened.

She listened as her husband, in over a hundred voices, cheered for her. She listened as his hands clapped from over a hundred locations. She listened as he called out in strange, sometimes comical but always exuberant, voices, "Teresa! Teresa! Hooray for Teresa! Good for you, Teresa! You've done it, Teresa!"

And this time . . . this time she heard.

She heard.

"I'm so sorry," Johann said. "I should never have done this. I'll erase it."

Teresa placed her hands on Johann's hands, looked up at him and said, "Actually, I like it. I like it. Let's leave it as it is."

I see Teresa from time to time. I see her in the grocery store or walking with her husband downtown. When I see her, I realize that I am looking at a miracle. I am looking at a human being who has overcome great suffering and rejection and found love, dignity and courage. Strangely, when I see Teresa—knowing what she has suffered, what she has overcome—I feel hope.

When I think of the many moments in my life that have been particularly painful, I wonder where God is. God can feel so absent in the world, absent from my work, absent from my many attempts to conjure love into my life. *Where is God?* my heart asks searchingly. Often, over time, I discover God has been waiting in the one place I am afraid to look. God is with me—deeply, intimately, with me. The painful truth is if I want to be with God, I often first have to be with myself. Like Teresa I have to look and see and feel my life with all of its failure. Like Jesus, I have to go and walk among the beggars, the blind, the lame, the outcasts, the angry, the sad, the frightened and lonely within me. This is where Jesus was found when he walked the earth. This is where he is still found—not only present in those hurting within my communities but also waiting to be received among the wounded within me.

These broken places within us are irresistible to God, and if I am willing to go and sit with these shamed and abandoned parts of myself, I sometimes hear the One who loves the world, calling my name in a hundred loving voices.

PRACTICE

Healing Past Wounds

Reflection

- In this chapter a husband tries to remake an experience that wounded his wife. Think of an experience in your past that caused you hurt or shame. Imagine watching that experience on video. What do you think you would notice if this experience were played back for you? Now imagine, like Teresa's husband, if you were to remake the video of this wounding experience. What images would you add or subtract, what sounds would you add or erase?
- When Teresa first watched the videotape of her law school graduation, she reacted with shame and anger to her husband's voice of love and encouragement. Who have been voices of encouragement and love in your life? How awkward or difficult has it been for you to receive love and compassion?

Action

- Take out pen and paper and write about an experience from your past that wounded you. Try to describe the experience as if you were an outside observer watching the experience take place. Leave space in the margins of your description. When you finish writing, take a few moments and then go back and read what you've written. As you read, think of the words that you wish you could have heard in that experience. Just as Teresa's husband dubbed his cheering voice onto the law school graduation video, what words would you like to say to your past self? Write these words in the margin of your description. What is it like to write these words? What is it like for the part of you that was hurt in that experience to hear these words now?

5

Women in Black

The Gift of Anger

I myself am the enemy most in need of healing.

Carl Jung

It's late March 2003 and the United States is buzzing with war. On every screen and radio fevered voices narrate the "shock and awe" firebombing of Baghdad. The long-anticipated US invasion of Iraq has begun. For weeks prior a group of fifteen to twenty women dressed only in black have stood in silent protest at the busiest intersection in our town of San Anselmo, thirty minutes north of San Francisco. In protest of the US march for war against Iraq, Women in Black have stood vigil across the United States and Europe, holding placards advocating for peace. The signs are simple: "Thou shall not kill." "Violence begets violence." "Will killing Iraqi children keep our children safe?"

The war and the lead-up to war has made me angry, fearful and cynical. I had recently heard a presentation by

UNICEF on how the US bombing of Iraqi water treatment plants in the 1991 Gulf War had caused the death of over half a million children. I knew (as is always the case) that women, children and civilians would bear the brunt of another Iraqi conflict. On the first weekend after the US invasion, the word spreads at the seminary where I work that the Women in Black are inviting men to join them in protest. Eager to do something with my frustration, I show up on a Sunday afternoon with a few other men from town, carrying my own poster colored by my two young sons. The placard reads "Love Your Enemy" in sunrise yellow, orange and red.

Before the vigil begins one of the women gathers us into a circle and invites us to say our names and state our reason for participating in the protest. I introduce myself and tell the group that as a Christian one of our primary values is to practice love toward others, including our enemies. Others give their names and reasons for joining the vigil. One of the women then reminds the group of the protocol: "Stand ten meters apart. Hold your placard. Remain silent. People may curse you, shout at you or seek to engage you in dialogue. Do not respond. Keep silence. Hold your placard. Our protest is in solidarity with all of those who have no voice. Our practice is to keep silent. Can everyone agree to these instructions?"

I nod my head with the others. The instruction is one I understand. For ten years I have been a practitioner of silent, contemplative prayer in the Christian tradition. I have taught classes in contemplation and Christian spiritual disciplines, and have written articles on the use of silence, solitude and Christian meditation with youth. The senior women invite the gathered group to stand in silence for five minutes before taking our places along the intersection. We stand, and the silence is rich and deep, connecting all of us to a common hope for peace. After five minutes the group disperses along the busy road.

I take a spot along the Sir Francis Drake Highway that runs from the interior towns and cities to the coast. The reactions of the passing drivers are mixed. Some honk horns and wave in support, others yell curses and flip the bird, most drive by without expression or simply look at us in confusion. The most awkward moments are when the stoplight turns red and a car halts just a few feet from the curb. The driver and passengers look at me, read the sign, then return their gaze forward while I stand, just a few feet away, awkwardly staring.

For the first hour of the afternoon protest I feel quite Christian and at times catch myself smiling and waving at drivers, secretly hoping that some student or colleague from the seminary might see me and think to themselves, *Look at Yaconelli over there standing peacefully, joyfully, in black clothes, with that colorful, childlike sign with the radical teachings of Jesus—while I'm sitting here in this polluting automobile, driving to the movies, eating a cheeseburger with extra bacon. Gosh, I wish I could be a model of spiritual living like Mark Yaconelli.*

And then suddenly, without warning, a red Toyota pickup stops directly in front of me, one lane back from the curb, and the driver, a man about my age, rolls down the passenger window, leans over so I can see his face and calmly calls to me, "Excuse me? Mr. Love Your Enemy? Do you have any idea what you're doing? Have you ever been to Iraq? You ever serve in the military? Do have any idea how much suffering Saddam has inflicted on his own people? Do you know what chemical weapons do to people? Do you know what happens when anthrax gets into your eyes and lungs? Hey, Mr. Peace and Love. You are an ignorant, f—— moron. Go home. You are making a fool out of yourself. You have no idea what you are doing. You have no idea what it takes to keep our country safe. Go home you stupid, ignorant a——!"

The whole time the man is speaking I'm looking at him and listening to him, and my mind is spinning in anger. *How dare this guy accuse me of ignorance! Does he have any idea how educated I am? A fool? He's the one making a fool out of himself. Iraqi chemical weapons are made with mustard gas, not anthrax! And yes, I know about the military. My brother's best friend died in another stupid, illegal operation in El Salvador. Who does this guy think he is?*

And then, before I know what's happening, I watch myself lower my sign, step off the curb, walk out between cars, place my face at the passenger window and say, "Are you calling me ignorant? You're the one who is ignorant! Do you believe whatever the television tells you? Do you know the US government has supported Saddam for decades? It's because of stupid, mindless people like you that we are killing . . ."

And then there's a hand on my shoulder. "Mark?" Cars are weaving around us, the driver is shouting back at me, the grip on my shoulder tightens. "Mark? Mark?" I hear the voice and feel the hand and snap my head around angrily expecting another confrontation, when I see the face of one of the elderly women. Her face pained, she looks at me with understanding eyes and says, "Mark? Mark, we hold silence. All right? I know you're upset, but we hold silence." She leans down to the window of the red truck driver and says, "I am sorry for my friend's outburst." The man says something dismissive and then drives off.

The woman places her hand on my back and walks me to the sidewalk. She stoops down, picks up her water bottle and offers me a drink. "Here. Drink some water." I set my sign down on the sidewalk. My body is shaking from the encounter. I drink with quivering hands, feeling shamed and silly, all of my spiritual hubris suddenly deflated. I hand back the bottle. I don't know what to do. The elderly woman picks up my sign and hands it to me. "Did your children make this?" I nod my head. "I like the colors." Again she places her hand on my back and then walks me to my place along the road. "When your children are upset, you pick them up and hold them until they become calm. Right? It doesn't help if you hold an upset child when you are upset."

She places her hands on mine. "We are here to hold suffering. Do you understand? We are here to hold the anger and fear and violence in us and in others until it feels understood and safe and transforms into trust. It's okay to be angry, but when the anger comes, just hold it, like a child who needs care, with love, all right? Just like it says on your sign. Hold your enemies. In silence and in love." And then she folds her hands behind her back, stands with her shoulder next to mine, and together we hold vigil amidst the kind and harried, resentful and confused, grateful and hostile faces.

Neuroscientists have recently begun to understand that for the human brain, vengeance is pleasurable. All of the bad feelings that rise up in response to an insult, past injuries or injustices (whether real or perceived) are suddenly released, and our emotional system is rebalanced when we are given the opportunity to lash out at others, even if we receive no practical benefit. Our anger seeks an opponent, a symbol, a stereotype, a stick man toward which to direct our pent-up fears and hurt. Often our "enemy" is eager to return the favor. And the (pleasurable) cycle of retribution turns and turns, seeking an eye for an eye until, as Gandhi noted, "everyone goes blind."

Much of Jesus' life and teachings are an attempt to break this cycle. Jesus does not return anger with anger. Jesus does not return the ridicule, the dehumanizing projections, the hatred and violence. Even at the point of death he refuses to demonize his persecutors, "Father, forgive them; for they do not know what they are doing" (Luke 23:34). Jesus seeks to listen beneath the anger and insult to the vulnerable desire that lies hidden within. He trusts that the anger masks a deep longing for acceptance, for healing, for dignity, for understanding and empathy.

When anger comes over me, rather than acting out, I am invited by Jesus to listen more deeply. The anger is only a cry that wants tending. Jesus trusts that at the level of the soul what my anger seeks most is justice. My anger wants my wounds honored and tended. My anger wants respectful relationships between people. My anger wants a world that protects the innocent. These are good desires, and my anger is most protective of these good desires.

The work that Jesus offers us is to recognize that the same is true of others. The anger mirrored in my enemy is also a cry for dignity, protection and safety. What if I could receive the anger of others as a cry for justice, a cry for respect, a cry for safety? What if I could see my own anger as a sign of God's yearning for right relationship? What if, like the Women in Black, every time I felt angry I stopped, stood still and listened more deeply?

PRACTICE

Listening to Anger

Reflection

- In recent days, what has made you angry? How do you carry this anger? To whom and in what way is this anger expressed? What is healthy and unhealthy about this anger?
- The woman in black reminds Mark that when one of his children is upset he holds them. Why is your anger upset? If you were to hold it like a child, what does it need (what actions, what words) before it could feel understood?

Action

- Find a place to pray imaginatively with your anger, some prayerful place where you won't be disturbed. Before you begin, take a few moments to read the story of Jesus encountering the Gerasene demoniac in Mark 5:1-20. The man is full of fear and rage, screaming and thrashing amidst the tombs until Jesus encounters him, listens to him and heals him. After reading the story take a moment to take a few breaths and fall into a prayerful silence. When you're ready, close your eyes and imagine your own anger to be a person in that story, living among the tombs. What would that person (that is, your anger) look like? How would the person be dressed? How would she or he behave?

- Take a few moments to simply allow your imagination to personify your anger. Now imagine Jesus or the presence of the Holy Spirit coming to be with this person (who represents your anger). Imagine Jesus saying to your anger, "What do you need?"
- Now listen. Without manipulating or forcing anything, simply listen to what your anger needs. What fear is your anger carrying? What longings does your anger harbor? For a few moments just listen, and if you feel drawn to it write down whatever comes to you.
- After you have listened, invite Jesus to come and be with this image, this person who represents your anger. In your imagination see if you might watch as Jesus comes and compassionately touches this part of you who longs to be seen and heard. For a few moments allow your anger to receive God's love and care. After dwelling in this space, see if there is some invitation for how God wants you to respond to this anger. Is there some action,

some awareness that God wants you to undertake as you move out from this prayer? Write down whatever comes to you. As your prayer time comes to a close, give thanks for whatever has occurred within your prayer and return your attention to the present time and space. As you move back into your daily life, try to be mindful of what your anger needs.

6

Initiation

The Gift of Powerlessness

Making the decision to have a child . . .
is to decide forever to have your heart
go walking outside your body.

Elizabeth Stone

The most difficult reality to accept is that everything changes. Nothing stays the same. No matter how much I try to keep everything I love safe and sound, there is no security. The tide takes everything away—even what I love. Life changes. And then changes some more. And then changes again. And my response is always to resist, resist, resist.

For example, children. My children. Two boys, one girl. My greatest treasures. When all is said and done, the center of my life has been my parenting years. It has felt as if my career, my marriage, our church participation, our home life, my weekend chores, my schedule and vacations have all been in service of creating a safe, nurturing, creative life for my children. And then everything changes. A son grows and looks outward, pining for the day when he can leave, depart, fling himself into the open world, without a map, without a guide, discarding all the comforts of childhood I've provided him.

Suddenly, I find myself powerless.

My parenting, my protection, my nurturing efforts are no longer needed, no longer wanted. I am left helpless and afraid. I begin to tell myself a story, a fearful story of what might happen to my children in a careless world, in an unpredictable future. And I begin to fall into an anxious, clinging worry—so much so that at times I am robbed of the very moments I could be enjoying with my children. I am robbed of reality until it strikes me that trusting my children (the heart of my heart) to God (particularly when one knows the stories of the Bible) is not foolish or naive.

On the occasion of my son Noah's thirteenth birthday, seven men (uncles, family friends, the lone grandfather) gathered to accompany him through his passage from childhood into adolescence. It was the last Saturday of November and we'd begun the day in our living room within a wide circle of extended family. After prayers, blessings and hugs, the men and Noah left the others and drove thirty miles up into the mountains outside of Ashland, Oregon.

While the men unpacked, Frank, an old family friend, hiked with Noah up to the highest mountain peak in the

Green Springs wilderness. They followed deer trails and logging roads while discussing Noah's hopes and fears about entering his teenage years. When they reached the summit, the autumn sun was an orange poppy, wilting across waves of firs, pines and oak trees. They paused to take in the descending sky, then Frank hugged my boy, handed him a journal full of soul-searching questions and spoke the final instructions, "When night falls and the stars begin to shine, look for a fire, then make your way. We'll be waiting."

On that clear November afternoon, Noah sat on the mountain and reflected on his childhood—what he would leave behind, what he would keep with him—then he wrote out his prayer for the coming year. He set his book down, sat on the highest rock he could find and silently waited for the stars to appear.

The sky darkened and Noah strained his eyes across the rolling forest, unsure which direction to look, certain the fire would be difficult to discern. What he didn't know was that the light would be unmistakable. A group of us had found a slash pile left by loggers that was as big as a three-bedroom house. As the first stars appeared, we eagerly stoked the embers of the dried manzanita branches, sage brush and pine boughs until the crusted sap and dead leaves ruptured into flames over seventy feet high.

Many hours after Noah had first entered the woods, we whooped and hollered as he came out from the shadows of the trees and entered the great circle of light from the roaring bonfire. We embraced him, sat him down near the warmth of the fire and handed the hungry boy a plate of meat and potatoes. "I'm glad to see you guys," were the first words he spoke.

That night the men took turns around the circle sharing the difficulties, pleasures and lessons learned from their own adolescent years. The stories, for the most part, were dark and uncensored—broken families, physical and emotional abuse, traumatic accidents, thoughts of suicide, loneliness, heartbreak and depression. Noah, whose childhood had been emotionally safe and loving, had no filter for the raw pain the men were disclosing. As the night deepened I watched Noah withdraw into himself. After a while he stopped making eye contact, and as the stories progressed, he pulled his knees in close to his chest. By the time we came to the last story, Noah was visibly feeling sick, his head bowed, his hands clenching his stomach. After the last man spoke, Noah walked to the edge of the clearing and began to wretch.

I knew immediately what was happening. The stories were too raw, too full of suffering. Noah was innocent. He had no way to integrate the hurt and confusion, no way to hold the unresolved pain. "Maybe it's food poisoning," one man suggested. But I knew differently. It was the exposure to human suffering. We packed up our things and made our way through the dark woods while Noah stopped from time to time to vomit. When we reached the cabin, I felt anxious and protective. "That's all for tonight," I announced.

Noah and I withdrew into a small bedroom with bunk beds. Noah lay silent on the upper bunk, curled in a fetal position. I lay beneath him unable to sleep, fearing that this initiation had overwhelmed him and worse, caused actual harm. Outside our room the men gathered around the cabin fireplace. The walls were thin and the surrounding forest silent, so their voices were audible. For some reason the conversation turned to stories of death and grief. Already anxious about Noah's disposition, I prayed the men would cease their dark conversation, knowing that Noah was also listening—and that the more he heard, the more sick we would both feel.

It wasn't until the early hours of the morning that the men retired and Noah drifted off to sleep. In the quiet that followed I sat and thought about what I had done. Unwittingly, I had exposed my son to the intimate reality of suffering and knew that his body, his heart, his spirit and mind were reeling. I felt swallowed up with anxiety, the same anxiety I felt those first nights after Noah was born when I lay awake listening to his breathing, feeling powerless to keep him safe.

It was just after sunrise when I heard Noah making his way down the bunk ladder. "How are you, son?" I asked.

"I feel good."

Relieved, I sat up and looked the boy over. "Really? You feel well?"

"Yeah, Dad. Do you want to play a game of Ping-Pong?" While the rest of the men slept, we walked through the brisk morning air to the cookhouse, where we'd spied an old Ping-Pong table. We played, and my heart was full of laughter as I glimpsed Noah's boyish smile. We returned to the cabin, where we found our group fixing the morning's breakfast.

We ate, packed the vehicles, and before descending the mountain the men encircled Noah and one by one gave him a blessing. We drove down into town and arrived at our church, where Noah's mom, younger siblings, aunts, cousins and grandmothers greeted him in the parking lot with hugs and kisses. During the service, just after the call to worship, Noah stood and read the day's Scripture and opening prayer. At the close of the service he was baptized, and as is our tradition, the pastor walked Noah slowly through the congregation as we sang John Carl Ylvisaker's "I Was There to Hear Your Borning Cry":

> I was there to hear your borning cry,
> I'll be there when you are old,
> I rejoiced the day you were baptized,
> to see your life unfold.

Around the pews Noah walked with great emotion as people stepped into the aisle to reach out and greet him with "Welcome Home." At one point his shy three-year-old cousin Easton noticed the emotion in Noah's eyes, leaned out of his mother's arms, wrapped his hands around Noah's neck and pressed his face against Noah's cheek. Immediately Noah began to cry. Watching my son weep, my wife and I fell to pieces—had this been too hard on him? Was this the right thing to do? We were full of uncertainty.

A year later I sat with an old friend who was experienced in Native American initiation ceremonies. I told Michael about my experience with Noah. When I got to the part about the men's talk of suffering and Noah's sickness, Michael nodded his head knowingly and said, "Sounds like the Spirit took over." I looked at him questioningly. "You wanted a safe passage for your son. You tried to control all the variables. You wanted a symbolic act, but the Spirit intervened. A young man's passage is always an awakening to suffering, learning to face and hold the darkness. It's about the parents' suffering as well—the parents learning to let go and trust their son, trust the larger community and trust God. This is what Mary ponders when Jesus escapes his family and sits with the elders in the temple as a young boy. This is what you were forced to ponder as well. Do you know the original meaning of the word *initiation*? It means 'entrance' or 'beginning.' This is his beginning into the work and suffering of adulthood. This is your entrance into the powerlessness you will now experience as he moves out from underneath your wing."

Two years after Noah was baptized, I was back on the same mountain with many of the same men, except our plans, once again, were hijacked by the Spirit. My sons are two years apart, and their birthdays are within a few days of one another, so again it was late November. This particular year, however, the weather was turbulent. For two weeks we'd had a series of storms that layered over a foot of snow across the mountains. Worried Route 66 would be impassable, we'd rounded up trucks with four-wheel drive and an assortment of tire chains. With limited visibility we made it up the twisting mountain road to the cabin. Once we arrived, we soon realized it was impossible to see, much less drive the logging roads that led back into the Green Springs Mountains. So, we improvised.

I called my friend Doug, who has lived on the Green Springs Mountains for over thirty years. Doug told me it was too dangerous to take Joseph up to the summit. He suggested we take the boy two miles up a road that branched off from the highway to a place where our family had lived for a year when Joseph was six. The site seemed ideal. Joseph would spend the afternoon and early evening in the woods, then make the journey down the country road to where we men would gather just across the empty highway.

We drove Joseph through the deep virgin snow and left him in a cluster of Douglas fir trees next to a creek where he had played as a child. It was early afternoon and the snow fell like lamb's wool from the gray sky. The woods were silent except for the creek creeping beneath a blanket of snow. Joseph was given a notebook for reflection and left to sit and pray among the trees. We hugged him and then gave him the instructions, "When night falls, follow the road back to the highway and look for a fire. We'll be waiting."

Five hours later we were surrounded by darkness. The men and I stood in a circle and watched as Doug sloshed diesel fuel across a frayed, upturned tweed couch that leaned shipwrecked atop a mound of discarded wood and mill ends. With careful tending, we managed to coax the fire to life. Each man stood stranded on rocks, trying to keep his feet out of the moat of melted snow around the bonfire.

About an hour after building the fire, my father-in-law spoke up, "Shouldn't Joseph be here by now?" By Doug's calculations it should have taken Joseph an hour to walk the two-mile road. The night was dark, the snow heavy. It was possible he had taken a wrong turn, become disoriented and headed up some driveway to a mountain cabin or followed a logger's switchback into the mountains.

"Should we look for him?" my friend Duane asked. "You know they spotted a mountain lion not far from here," he offered unhelpfully. Resisting the fear I felt welling inside, knowing that the struggle, my powerlessness and anxiety were part of the ritual, I tried to calm the group and myself, "He'll be here. The snow's thick on the road. It's just taking longer than we estimated."

Another forty minutes passed. The phone rang. I reached in my pocket, upset that I'd left my ringer on. It was my wife. I knew she was worried by the storm and wanted assurance that Joseph was safe, but what could I tell her? I switched it off. A minute later my brother-in-law's phone rang. "Don't answer it," I called across the fire. "She'll only be more frightened if she hears he's not here."

Jack looked at me and shrugged, "She's my sister. I have to answer."

He picked up the phone and we all listened, "No, he's not here. No, we're not searching. Yeah, it's still snowing." Jack pulled the phone from his ear, "She wants to talk to you."

I took the phone. Her voice was tight, frightened. I listened to my wife's anxiety. I felt my own fears rising up, but something deep within told me this was part of it. This was the Spirit allowing us to feel the fear and pain of letting go, of trusting our son, of trusting God, of knowing that Joseph is growing up and will enter many situations that we can't control or manage. "Listen," I said as calmly as I could. "He's a smart kid. He's strong. This is part of what's to come. We need to wait and trust." Jill was uncertain—and so was I.

I promised her if he didn't show up in thirty minutes we'd start searching.

We waited. It had now been dark for nearly three hours. Joseph was two hours past the time we had calculated. My father-in-law spoke, "Isn't there a millpond next to the highway? It's covered by snow. It probably looks like a vacant field. Joseph might've tried to cross it and fallen in." Now the group was alarmed and began to consider all the negative possibilities. Some left the fire and tried to peer across the darkness. Other men tried to assess whether the pond might be an actual danger.

Half the group had resolved to search for my son, but for some reason, for some unexplainable reason, my heart was full of trust. I trusted Joseph. Despite the knowledge that things go wrong, kids get hurt, tragedy happens, still I trusted. Remembering the words of my friend Michael, I trusted that the fear and the unknowing were part of the change that was taking place. This was the initiation.

"Let's stay here," I said as firmly as I could. "He'll make it."

The men went silent. Thirty minutes passed. The phone began to ring. "It's Jill!" my father-in-law announced.

I walked over to the phone, carefully preparing my words, when someone cried out, "There he is!" We looked across the mill yard and saw a tall, dark outline leaning forward into the wind and falling snow. He was about a hundred yards from us, moving slowly, his legs calf-deep in white.

"Tell Jill he's here," I called to my father-in-law. We stood relieved and smiling at the edge of the fire as Joseph shuffled toward us. He entered the firelight and we noticed his pants were soaked, but his face was beaming. He raised his hands in victory, "I made it!" he announced. One by one we embraced him and patted him on the back. Then we anxiously waited to hear his story.

"I could hardly see the road through the snowfall. I walked with my head down trying to make sure I didn't go off the road. It was silent, but every once in a while I heard this small sound of rattling keys. I knew someone with a keychain must be following me. I prayed and prayed for God to protect me. Eventually I got the courage to stop and turn around, but as soon as I did the noise stopped, and the person following me stayed still, just out of sight. At one point I got scared and started running. I ran and ran, but I could hear the keys jangling faster, as if the person was running too. Through the trees I saw the lights of a house and decided to turn and ask for help. I ran across this field, and then all of a sudden I fell. I fell into a ditch, probably some irrigation ditch, that was waist deep with water. Still frightened and shocked by the freezing water, I quickly climbed up the bank. As I climbed out I noticed the zipper on my backpack made the same noise as the rattling keys. Then I realized what was happening. There was no one after me. It was just the sound of my zipper jangling as I walked. It took me a while to find the road back to the highway, but eventually I did. I walked the rest of the way thinking about how I had created my own fear and how I'd almost seriously hurt myself running from it. I started to get really cold, but then I saw the fire glowing through the trees, and I just started smiling, knowing that all of you were waiting."

We went back to the cabin and Joseph peeled off his wet clothes and sat in front of the fireplace while we ate dinner. He sat and listened as the men told stories from their own teen years, stories of heartbreak, fear and uncertainty. Joseph listened carefully, but he was so grateful to be dry and safe that the suffering stories didn't seem to disturb him. After each man had said his piece, Joseph asked if we could play some music. We broke out guitars and harmonicas, mandolins and violins, drums and ukuleles, and belted out the words to the Waterboys' "Fisherman's Blues."

The next morning the sun was shining and the world was soft and white. We chained up the trucks and made the slow trek out of the mountains and down into town, where once again our extended family met us at the entrance to our church. Joseph was mobbed with hugs and kisses, and then he went and sat in the first pew between his sister and brother. At the close of the service he was baptized. And what struck me most were the final words of our pastor's prayer.

Her hand on his head, she prayed, "May God bless you and keep you, today and all the days of your life." That was the moment I felt the release. All my anxiety, all my worry, all my fears as a parent had come up against the raw truth that I was powerless. I do not have the power to keep my children safe. I do not control their physical, emotional or spiritual lives. My faith in God does not keep me from tragedy and suffering. My love for God will not keep my children from disease or violence or tragedy. But what I can do, what lives in me deeper than my anxiety and helplessness, is trust. I trust God. I trust my children. And I trust my own capacity to love. And for some reason, at that moment, hearing the deep yearning of my heart out loud—*May God bless you and keep you, today and all the days of your life*—I trusted. I discovered that in the midst of my helplessness, my heart trusts. And that trust, that faith is enough. And God is enough. No matter what befalls my children in this life, God will hold them and keep them and bless them.

Joseph then went to the piano and played a song he had composed for the occasion. He sat there in a red dress shirt with a black vest and black pants, his hair wild and wiry. His song began with a childlike melody that grew in complexity, speed and power. He pressed his foot down on the brass pedals and pounded out a cascade of beautiful, heartfelt chords. He played and played, and as he played I began to weep—with gratitude that Joseph was safe, with gratitude that God had given me this boy who was now on his way to becoming a man, with gratitude that the Spirit was teaching me to resist my parental fear and anxiety, and trust that the sons we had raised would grow into men, men who can be trusted to find their way home.

PRACTICE

Letting Go

Reflection

- Everything changes. What changes are you undergoing in your life that you have no power over? What reactions are you having within yourself in response to these changes? Now reflect on what is unchanging in you and the world. What parts of yourself, your life, your faith can you depend on and hold onto (your love for your family, the presence of God, experiences of grace)?

- The story in this chapter is about a rite of passage. What rite of passage are you being invited to take at this time in your life? Mark's friend tells him that an initiation is an "entrance" or "beginning." What new aspect of life is the Spirit seeking to initiate you into? What are you being asked to let go of? What are you being asked to embrace?

Action

- One of Jesus' last words recorded in Scripture is the prayer he prays while suffering helpless on the cross: "Into your hands I commit my spirit" (Luke 23:46 NIV). Take a few moments to sit in a prayerful place. After allowing a quiet to descend on you, simply repeat this phrase within you: "Into your hands I commit my spirit." Repeat this phrase as different loved ones, different situations in the world, different aspects of your own life come into your own awareness: "Into your hands I commit my spirit." Allow yourself to pray for your own powerlessness again and again, responding in trust: "Into your hands I commit my spirit." When you encounter situations that are out of your control, situations that draw out your own fearful anxiety, return to these words, repeating them over and over until you begin to develop a sense of trust and spaciousness.
- Each of us has things we cling to (a sense of self, a loved tradition, people, places, etc.). At the same time, each of us is being asked to let go of certain things. Reflect on a rite of passage that you sense the Spirit is seeking to

bring you through. See if you might create a ritual that would help you mark this passage. Maybe it's a night alone in some deserted place (a monastery, a campsite, a cabin in the woods). Maybe there is a pilgrimage that you could undertake to practice walking toward this new life (a hiking trip, a sacred pilgrimage walk, a journey toward a sacred place in your life). You might have others accompany you or pray for you or receive you at the end of this ritual. The ritual might be private or shared within a community. See if this physical marking of an interior change helps you to let go of the old life and receive the new life that God is bringing you.

7

The Ungrieved Grief

The Gift of Loss

Sorrow is so woven through us, so much a part of our souls, or at least any understanding of our souls that we are able to attain, that every experience is dyed with its color. That is why, even in moments of joy, part of that joy is the seams of ore that are our sorrow. They burn darkly and beautifully in the midst of joy, and they make joy the complete experience that it is. But they still burn.

Christian Wiman

It is a hot, muggy week in July and six thousand Presbyterian teenagers from across the United States and abroad are gathered for a conference. The theme of the conference is hope.

After twelve months of planning, the event leaders have brought together a talented group of actors, musicians, videographers, multimedia artists, liturgists, preachers and teachers. Together, this well-meaning group has designed and led worship services filled with attention-grabbing images, dramatic words, heart-moving songs, creative games and relevant biblical teaching. The students and youth leaders love it. The mood of the conference is positive and upbeat. Like a rock show, people crowd eagerly outside the doors an hour before each service and sing songs, hit beach balls, laugh and joke in an atmosphere of fun and frivolity.

On the third night of the conference a celebrated preacher is flown in to address the gathering. "God loves you! Be hopeful!" was his enthusiastic refrain as he summed up the message of the week.

The year is 2007, and the United States is deep into the Iraq War. President George W. Bush has just announced that he will send an additional 33,000 American soldiers into Iraq. That same week newspapers report a new study claiming that over 160,000 Iraqi civilians have been killed since the start of the war. This is our daily news in the United States.

Meanwhile, "God loves you! Be hopeful!"

At each evening worship service a youth group from a different part of the country is invited to make a presentation. Some youth groups sing. Other groups enact dramatic readings. On the second-to-last night of the conference, right after standing to sing "Our God Is an Awesome God," a youth group stands shoulder to shoulder on the soft-lit stage and offers a meditation, in the Presbyterian tradition, on our confession of sin. The group introduces themselves and then says, "This is a video we made about the Iraq War." The house lights dim and up onto the video screens are projected images of wounded, maimed and sometimes dead Iraqi children. There is no narrative—only a recording of a children's choir singing "Jesus Loves Me, This I Know."

The images are gut-wrenching. Particularly disturbing is the accompanying syrupy, surreal soundtrack. Onto the screen appears a four-year-old girl in a white dress. She has no arms. The scar tissue at her shoulders is red and tender. She stares out from the screen with large, blank eyes. The image fades and into focus comes a picture of a two- or three-year-old boy. He is lying in a bomb crater surrounded by broken concrete. His head and eyes are wrapped in a torn shirt soaked in blood. The images move slowly, contemplatively, while through the speakers we hear a choir of children singing in happy, enthusiastic voices

Little ones to him belong;
They are weak but he is strong!
Yes, Jesus loves me!
Yes, Jesus loves me!
Yes, Jesus loves me!
The Bible tells me so!

Matched to the images, the song feels like a cruel mockery, as if the joyful singers are taunting the wounded children, "See how Jesus loves you? See how our strong Jesus treats you little ones?"

The song ends. The images cease. The lights are raised in the auditorium, and the audience sits stunned as the youth group simply exits. The stage sits empty for an awkward minute, and then someone cues the worship band and we stand, somewhat disoriented, and begin to sing another upbeat song of praise. My ten-year-old son, Joseph, unable to ignore what he has witnessed grabs my arm, "Dad, I need to throw up." As we hurry out of the building, Joseph's elder brother whispers an explanation, "I think it was those pictures, Dad."

That night, as Joseph lay curled on his bed, my sons try to process what they've seen. "Why did they show those pictures in worship? Why are we bombing children in Iraq? Why aren't Christians trying to stop the war? Why doesn't God protect them?" Talking with my sons I suddenly feel how false and empty the conference has been. A year of planning, five days of teaching, five days of prominent Christian preachers, five days of creative dramas, five days of celebrity Christian bands, five days of enthusiastic hope in God—all suddenly erased by a three-minute montage of real suffering. We have been fooling ourselves. The week's activities have been an escape from reality, a kind of happy pretending. There can be no real hope, no Christian hope, without acknowledging the reality of death. There can be no real hope unless it somehow embraces, unashamedly, the presence of real suffering in the world.

The next day I gather a random group of forty students and tell them my insight. They agree that the images of hurting children has somehow challenged all the teaching of the week. The students are feeling helpless, uncertain how to relate to such bottomless suffering. We take out our Bibles, we talk about our own encounters with suffering, and together we craft a service that is willing to face grief.

The first thing we do is ask the organizers to hold the service outside, on a hillside, under the stars, away from the slick auditorium with its multimedia screens, state-of-the-art sound system and theater lights. If we are to meet the real God in the midst of real suffering we need to be in a real place.

Just after sunset, with the six thousand youth and adult leaders sitting outside on a warm summer night, I walk to the microphone and remind the group of the images we have all seen of the wounded children from Iraq. I talk about the shame, embarrassment, distress and horror that many of the students have shared with me in response to the images. I wonder out loud about our capacity to hope, to trust God's love, when innocent children are dying, recalling that Jesus knew how to be in relationship to pain and death. I suggest that if we are to bring hope to the wounded and dying in this world, then, like Jesus, we have to be willing to enter into suffering. We have to be willing to be honest about our own suffering, our own wounds, our own grief, as well as the suffering that exists within the world.

I gently suggest that although the conference has been about hope, we have forgotten the first step. We have forgotten to talk about hopelessness, despair and death. The resurrection comes after the crucifixion. We do not become hopeful by talking about hope. We become hopeful by entering darkness and waiting for the light. We become hopeful by being honest with one another about our pain and then waiting, together, for God to show us a way toward healing.

As planned, one by one a group of twenty young people come to the microphone and name a form of suffering in their community as well as what they believe the people in their community are waiting for. As these sufferings are named, students are invited to stand (and remain standing) if they, or someone they love, share that particular affliction or despair. Here are some of their statements:

"I come from Northern Canada. In my community we are suffering from alcoholism. We are waiting to be freed from addiction."

"I'm from Detroit. In my town young people are shooting each other. We are waiting for someone to show us how to stop the killing."

"I come from Serbia. In my town we're still filled with lots of hatred toward our enemies. We don't know what we are waiting for . . . I think it's peace."

"I live in a little town in Indiana. People don't have jobs, and we don't know how to help one another. We're waiting to make friends."

"I'm from Los Angeles. I know lots of kids who are suffering from sexual abuse. I'm also trying to heal from sexual abuse. I am angry all the time. I guess we're waiting for someone to listen."

"I'm from South Carolina. We have an army base and lots of military families who have soldiers in Iraq and Afghanistan. Some of them have killed and hurt people, sometimes innocent civilians, but they don't want to talk about it. We are waiting for healing and peace."

The night is dark and moonless. The only light is from the stars and a large circle of candles placed around a fifteen-by-twenty-five-foot wooden cross that lies at the foot of the hillside. After each person comes to the microphone, a young man raises a hammer and strikes the cross, causing a loud thud to echo across the hillside. The crowd remains silent and prayerful, the sound of the hammer representing a cry from all who are in pain.

As people on the hillside quietly stand up in solidarity, the young boy assigned to strike the cross begins to swing the hammer with all his might, overwhelmed by the palpable reality of suffering that night. With anger and sadness and frustration he hits the cross again and again and again and again and again—for the terrible mystery and reality of human pain, addiction, abuse, violence, despair and death. Bang . . . bang . . . bang the hammer falls, at times splintering the cross beams while thousands stand silent, helpless, bearing witness to the dark truth. We stand and stand, allowing the hammer blows to ring through us, until finally, exhausted, emotionally drained and out of breath, the young man tosses the hammer to the ground and walks away, his head hung in despair.

The hillside is suddenly silent and you can hear people quietly weeping. Then a voice from somewhere in the crowd begins to hum "Amazing Grace." Slowly, carefully, she makes her way down through the crowd, humming more loudly now and gathering other young women along the way. They walk down to the foot of the hillside, pick up the votive candles and then encircle the cross in candlelight. They stand, humming in unison as more students come forward, enter the circle of light and lift the cross onto their shoulders. Accompanied by the candle bearers, they walk into the crowd of broken, stuck, hurting people. The procession slowly, solemnly passes, like a funeral march, through the crowd until they reach the middle of the hillside where they stop and lay the cross on the grass.

Each person had been given a small unlit candle as they came to the service, and now those gathered around the cross turn and light the candles of those standing next to them. Those students then turn and light the candles of those next to them until the light begins to move from the cross along the hillside. As the candles are lit, we all begin to sing, "Amazing Grace, how sweet the sound . . ." On and on we sing as the light spreads among the searching, hopeless, addicted, abused, angry, lost, faithless, suffering followers of Jesus.

That night, under the starlit sky, we were all, every one of us, overcome with hope—not the idea of hope, not the theological principle of hope, but the reality of hope—the living hope, the eternal hope, the hope that can never be quenched, the hope that has overcome death, the hope that waits to be discovered within the darkness and despair of every human heart. Through a night of despair we had begun to discover a way of life.

If I were to name the suffering that exists in the West, it is ungrieved grief. It is an unwillingness to admit, to name, to embrace the pain of loss. Many of the destructive practices of the Western world can be traced to a desire to distract ourselves from grief, what we're missing, what we've lost.

Distracted from the reality of suffering, my heart hardens and I lose my capacity for compassion, I become less alive.

"Loss is the great teacher," Elisabeth Kübler-Ross once wrote. Without a willingness to face loss, I learn nothing. I spin in circles. I hide from others. I repeat my mistakes. I become numb to suffering. I lose my capacity for compassion and joy. I shield my heart from the presence of God—the God of Jesus, the God who suffers, the God who weeps and the God who laughs.

And yet I can't force my heart to enter into grief. Sometimes the pain is too much, the loss so great that I have to approach it sideways, slowly, with gentleness and care. I have to wait until I know I am safe, wait until I find trusted friends who can keep me from falling into an abyss of despair. But when friends are found, when my heart is safe, when my soul is ready, then I find grief, lament, to be the deepest experience of prayer—to sit in the darkness, sit in the midst of my own gaping wounds, sit within the reality and absurdity of death, sit until light comes, sit until singing comes, sit until I sense the hand of the Pain Bearer, the Life Giver, the Compassionate One, coming to my aid, helping me to shoulder the weight.

PRACTICE

Holding Hope

Reflection

- In the ritual students were asked to name the suffering in their communities. What sufferings live unnamed within your own community? What sufferings live unnamed within your family? What are the unnamed sufferings that live within you? Now as you reflect on each of these, what is each of these sufferings waiting for?

- It is understandable that each of us wants to avoid grief, not only because we want to keep ourselves safe from the pain of loss but also because we don't want to fall into despair at the meaninglessness often surrounding death and loss. Do you notice yourself avoiding facing some of your own losses? Do you notice you are protecting yourself from "ungrieved grief"? Why? What are the good reasons for keeping yourself away from facing the losses of your life? By avoiding facing these losses what is gained or how are you harmed?
- The great scholar of death and dying, Elisabeth Kübler-Ross, once wrote, "Loss is the great teacher." What have you learned from your experiences of loss? What gifts have you been given in the midst of loss?

Action

- One of the most ancient practices within the Christian tradition is to pray for tears. Tears, in our common Christian history, were seen as a sign of the Holy Spirit and the wellspring from which all prayer springs forth. If you feel drawn to it, find a safe place where you can pray for tears. Once you have found a sacred place, bring an unlit candle and place it before you.
- Now allow yourself to become aware of God's compassionate presence. For a few moments simply allow yourself to be aware of and in relationship with the God who holds all sorrows. If it's helpful, you might picture the presence of Jesus next to you.

- After a period of rest and quiet, allow yourself to reflect on the sorrows of the world. Let your attention fall on the various sufferings that have come to your attention in recent days—wars, the neglect and destruction of the earth, the plight of refugees, the poor in your community, the conflict within your family. Allow the Spirit to bring you images of various faces, situations and sufferings that you are aware of.
- As various situations come to you, allow sorrow to rise up from the depths of your heart for the hurting and broken. Like a tender mother holding her wounded child, let yourself hold these pained situations, allowing your heart to expand and break open in compassion for what they are suffering.
- If it feels right, see if you might share God's own tears for those who are helpless and hurting. Pray for tears. Let yourself weep and hurt for all who feel abandoned, unloved, discarded, pained and alone. For as long as it feels right, share God's suffering and the suffering of those who you are called to pray with.
- After a time of grieving, light the candle. Light the candle as a symbol of God's light, God's love, God's presence that seeks to bring an end to darkness, to ignorance, to selfishness and cruelty. Take a few minutes to sit quietly and gaze on this small light. Let yourself be comforted and accompanied by this light that no darkness can extinguish.
- When you're ready, picture this flame warming those who are cold and abandoned, imagine this flame shining

within each hurting heart, holding hope and comfort for all who are suffering.

- End your prayer by giving thanks for the lives of those who have come to you in prayer. Then listen to see if there is some way the Spirit is calling you to respond, some way you are being asked to act on behalf of those you have been praying for.

8

The Accident

The Gift of Suffering

The most beautiful people we
have known are those who have known
defeat, known suffering, known struggle,
known loss, and have found their
way out of those depths.

Elisabeth Kübler-Ross

It is another workday morning for the London accountant, another day of downtown traffic, when, as commonly happens, there is a call on the cell phone. The ringtone jangling for his attention, his eyes focused on the road ahead, the accountant instinctively reaches into his coat pocket just as he has done a thousand times before. The pocket is empty. He checks his pants. Nothing. He glances over at the passenger seat. Not there either. While making his way through the busy morning commute, one hand searches the center storage bin and cup holders.

Empty. On and on the singing phone beckons—it might be his wife or his children calling from school. It might be his friend wanting to rehash last night's dinner party or a client looking to reschedule an appointment.

The man weaves the car around a parked delivery truck, then tilts his head and listens. Aha! The phone has fallen to the floor. He gives the traffic a quick scan then swipes his hand over the matted carpet. Vacant. He bends his wrist and reaches under his seat until his fingertips brush the cool, round plastic edge of the phone. Yes! He scoots to the edge of his chair, lowers his right shoulder, stretches his arm and lets his fingers, crablike, carefully enfold the . . . *thump*! The car heaves violently over the curb and onto the sidewalk. He jerks himself up, his hands pull at the wheel, his feet searching, stomping for the brake when *thud*! A body. A man. A wash of black hair pressed in an instant, infinite moment against the glass.

"We've all done it," my friend James tells me. "You reach for a bagel. You glance at a map. You turn a dial. You take your eyes off the road and expect nothing unusual to happen." James works as the director of restorative justice on the island of Guernsey, one of the British Channel Islands just thirty miles from the Normandy coast in France. He spends most of his time working in the local prison, creating situations where perpetrators face their crimes and are reconciled with victims.

The work is emotionally grueling and often heartbreaking. James sits with murderers, rapists and other violent criminals, helping them face their past, their emotional wounds, the violence they've perpetrated and the harm it has done to others. After many hours of counseling, his work often culminates with a face-to-face meeting between a perpetrator and a victim. In these meetings the perpetrators listen as the victims tell their story of the pain they have suffered. Then the perpetrator seeks to make restitution.

Curious about his reconciliation work, I've asked James to tell me if there is any redemption in suffering. He pauses for a moment, then tells me of a case mediated by Andrew, a friend of his. "It was an accident. A driver on his way to work. The cell phone rang. He reached down to the floorboard. The car jumped the curb and hit a man. The victim was rushed to a hospital. The driver was taken to jail."

"It's the kind of thing that could happen to any of us," James says somberly. I listen, thinking of the many times I've answered a cell phone, read map directions, reached for food, even changed shirts while driving. He's right. It's only luck to have not ended up in an accident.

James continues the story. The victim goes into a coma. He's put on life support. He has a wife and a six-year-old boy. The doctors tell the wife that there is no chance for recovery. There is virtually no brain activity. His organs are badly damaged. It is only the ventilators, dialysis machines and heart monitors that sustain his life. Despite this information the wife and boy stay at the hospital praying for a miracle. She reads to her husband, whispers in his ear, has her son sing and read his favorite books out loud. She massages her husband's feet and hands and gathers friends and family to pray around the bed. But nothing changes.

After a month the doctors sit down with the wife and show her the brain scans and other tests. "He is in a vegetative state. He is being kept alive by machines. There is no hope for recovery." The wife knows her husband would not want this. She goes home and reconciles herself to the awful reality—her husband is not coming back.

The next afternoon she and her son go to the hospital where she announces her excruciating decision. She explains to her son what is about to take place—the hospital staff will turn off the ventilator and heart monitors, and they will let their beloved husband and father go. The boy backs away from his mother and screams in protest, "You can't do this! Don't let him die!" The boy climbs up onto his father's bed and lays his body across him. He presses his face against his father's chest, wraps his small arms around his neck and sobs.

Patiently, gently, lovingly, the mother waits by the bed of her dying husband and inconsolable son until eventually, reluctantly, the boy allows his mother to hold his limp and grieving body while the ventilator and heart monitors are switched off. In the silence that follows, the man's body takes a few short, shallow breaths, then emits a long, final exhale. The heart slows to a stop, the room goes mute, and the man dies.

"My friend Andrew is standing outside the hospital room with a policeman," James tells me, his voice filled with emotion. "The mother rocks her son while they both cry and cry. The scene is absolutely heartbreaking."

The woman and her son finally exit the hospital room. The policeman informs the young widow that the driver is in custody and will be prosecuted for manslaughter. The woman asks about the driver—who he is, where he lives. Then she asks, "How is he?"

Andrew, who has been visiting the driver in jail, says to her, "He's a mess. He wants to kill himself. We have him on suicide watch."

"I want to see him," the woman replies. Andrew tells her that he can make arrangements for a future meeting. "I want to see him now," she insists. Andrew makes a call to the jail. The woman tenderly hands her son over to her parents, then rides with Andrew to the jail.

They drive in silence. Shackled and dressed in prison clothes, the accountant is waiting in the prison's visitor room when they arrive. The young widow enters the room, sits across from the man who killed her husband and the father of her son and says, "I want to tell you about my husband." With deep pain in his eyes the accountant listens. He listens as the woman tells the story of her husband's life—who he was, how he was loved, what he meant to her and her son.

At times the widow is overwhelmed with grief and breaks into tears. Each time this happens, the accountant weeps along with her. The woman finally finishes and goes silent. She drops her head and sits with shoulders slumped, her body empty and drained. She sits a while, then finally draws herself together, takes a deep breath and turns her attention to the remorseful prisoner. "They tell me you want to kill yourself." The man looks at the woman with red-rimmed eyes. "Is that true?" the widow asks.

In a quiet but steady voice he answers, "Yes, it's true."

The woman sits and searches the man's face, his eyes. Then she stands, walks over, clasps her hands on his shoulders, pulls him up to his feet and embraces him. She holds the man who killed her husband and whispers into his ear, "There's been enough dying. I want you to live."

The accountant falls apart, crying uncontrollably as the young widow holds him. When he finally is able to contain himself, the woman steps back, looks at him one last time and says definitively, "It was an accident." She turns and, without another word, walks away.

James lowers his head and wipes the tears from his eyes as I do the same. "The woman has to return to an empty house. She has to raise a wounded and grieving son. She has to make a living as a single parent. She had every right to demand vengeance, every right to scream and pour out her anger at the careless driver. But she didn't. She chose to offer kindness. She chose forgiveness. She chose to keep the damage of this horrible accident from destroying another life."

James then turns to address the question I've brought to him, "You want to know what suffering can make possible in a person? Grace. Compassion. Forgiveness. Every human being has this ability to love and forgive. I have witnessed people who have suffered violence, people raised by abusive parents, people who live in the most oppressive social conditions, people without education or resources. I've watched these people suddenly embody this mysterious capacity to care, to love, to forgive. You have to know that's possible in people. You have to know that possibility waits within each of our sufferings—to be healers, to be healed."

Many of us find ourselves living within a small sliver of our humanity. We live as caricatures of ourselves, spending most of our energy and attention on physical cravings, emotional reactions, anxieties about the future and repetitive internal judgments. We spend weeks, months, even years of our lives grasping after some elusive success, until we almost lose touch with our capacity for gratitude, for kindness, for humor and joy.

And then life is shattered. Death. Injustice. Betrayal. And if we stop and notice, it is possible to recognize that all the anxieties, all the fears, all the worries about our career, our possessions, our Internet provider have turned to smoke. Overwhelmed by grief, we are sometimes given moments of clarity, that the life we spent most of our energy maintaining was simply an anxious illusion, taught to us by an anxious culture.

Baptized by suffering, our eyes can be opened, our heart opened, our soul awakened from its slumber. In this moment no one needs to remind us of repentance, for we are overwhelmed with regret for wasted time, wasted worry, all the meaningless tasks that distracted us from the deeper soundings within our soul for presence, for relationship, for beauty, for thankfulness. And suddenly, strangely, we discover a deep yearning to be with those who suffer, a yearning to repent for injuries we've inflicted, an ache to honor those we have lost by loving more fearlessly.

The suffering is unwanted, unjust, unwelcome, but now that it is here, we find that within its brutal, destructive, purposeless presence comes a gift. Somehow this same repulsive suffering has uncovered a great spring of compassion within our hidden heart—a spring we could not have discovered if not for the devastation we have undergone. And although it feels blasphemous, and although we wish the suffering away, at the same time we find ourselves giving thanks for the gift that we have been given.

We are softer now.

We are open now.

We are human now.

And when the suffering releases its grip, when we are able to glimpse the gift of this world, the gift of our lives, the gift of one another, we discover, possibly for the first time, our great power to love and be loved. We find ourselves nodding, not with belief but with understanding, when the Teacher says, "Unless a grain of wheat falls to the earth and dies, it remains just a single grain" (John 12:24). And we find ourselves capable of moving, even in the midst of horror, traveling out toward the prison, walking into the jail cell, embracing the one who has shattered our lives, whispering from the dark, fertile forest of our being, "Live. I want you to live."

PRACTICE

Seeking Healing

Reflection

- Recall a moment of suffering from your past, something at least five or ten years back in time. As you reflect on this experience take out a piece of paper and make a list of what was lost or damaged through this experience. Now, on the other side of the paper make a list of the gifts you received from this experience. What do you notice about these lists? How has this event brought you either closer to or further from God? What actions might you want to undertake as you look at what has been lost and what has been given through this experience?

- We can't force our hearts to forgive. We can only create situations that are more vulnerable to the gift of forgiveness. In this chapter it's important for the grieving widow to go to the prison in person. Once there, she first needs the prisoner to know how much she loved her husband. How important is it for a victim's suffering to be heard by a perpetrator in order for real forgiveness to take place? Do you believe the woman would have been able to forgive the driver if he had not shown tears and empathy?
- In the story James says, "I have witnessed people who have suffered violence, people raised by abusive parents, people who live in the most oppressive social conditions, people without education or resources. I've watched these people suddenly embody this mysterious capacity to care, to love, to forgive. You have to know that's possible in people. You have to know that possibility waits within each of our sufferings—to be healers, to be healed." What is it that would allow you to authentically forgive yourself or another person? What is it that you need in order to forgive those who have harmed you?

Action

- It is difficult to ask for help. Sadly, this is particularly true within the church. Whether we are ministers or laypeople, it is difficult to admit our own suffering. And yet part of growing spiritually is accepting our need for love and care. Spend some time praying about a suffering you have been carrying for a while. What do you need in order to address this suffering at this time in your life? Maybe it is a conversation with a trusted friend. Maybe it is to join a group of people who have undergone a similar suffering. Maybe it is to begin to write out your own thoughts and feelings about this issue so you can see and hear what your heart needs. Take some time to simply ask God, "What do I need in order to heal?" And then trust what emerges.

9

THE DARK NIGHT

The Gift of Darkness

It is only that blind faith that carries me through for in reality to me all is darkness.

The silence and the emptiness is so great that I look and do not see, listen and do not hear.

MOTHER TERESA

I CAN'T STOP THINKING ABOUT the beginning, the romance, the way God felt in my heart, in my body, when I first began ministry. There was no need to study, to prepare, all I had to do was open my mouth and let my heart spill over with love. My soul was a greenhouse growing with faithful words, images, feelings and insights.

But that was before.

Now, years into ministry my heart is a dustbowl, my mouth chalk. And God? God is as silent as stone. I turn to Scripture for help, but the words offer no comfort. The Bible reads like an artifact, the verses rinsed of color. And where is my prayer, that secret communication with God? I call out to God, but in return I hear only the empty echo of my own longing. It's not that God has ceased to exist—it's more personal than that. God has abandoned me.

What's particularly damning is that this is my vocation. I'm a professional Christian. I can't afford to let God go AWOL. God is my job. God is my identity. I need faith, a living faith, in order to have some kind of warmth to radiate to those I serve. But no matter what I try, I can't work it up. I buy books, attend conferences, go on retreat and force myself to engage in spiritual exercises, but the truth is it all seems like a charade. None of it works. God has abandoned me, and I'm left only with the longing and the haunting memories of what was.

In the year 2000 I was running home from work one afternoon to change clothes and pack my suitcase. I was flying out to direct a retreat for a group of educators at the World Council of Churches. The organizers of the event had called me at the last minute and asked me to come, even though they had no money to cover my expenses. Believing this was God's directing, I bought my own ticket, booked one of my few precious weekends and was hustling to catch a plane. I showered, packed and started to head out the door when my two sons, just four and two years old, hugged my legs and began to cry. I looked over at my wife for help and then noticed that she too had eyes filled with tears. "Why do you keep leaving?" she asked me. Feeling emotionally overwhelmed, I exclaimed, "I don't have a choice! I have to go!"

"You do have a choice," my wife responded gently. "But you keep choosing the same thing." Angry, saddened, feeling tired and drained, I peeled my sons from my legs, looked helplessly at my wife and ran out to a waiting taxi. During the drive to the airport I felt empty and discouraged. "I don't have a choice!" I had shouted. When had God become a tyrant? I thought of my sons and the heartbreak in their eyes, and then memory struck and I began to recall so many times when I had watched my own father abandon our family week after week after week throughout my childhood. I sat on the plane to Chicago and felt my faith drain out from my feet. How could a person committed to silence, solitude and presence spend his life so scattered, so full of self-promotion? I suddenly realized that what was driving my life was not God but a mixture of wounds and desires. What I had named as God was not God.

In the weeks that followed, my prayer life went vacant. I worked at a seminary, and each morning I sat with staff members as we did *lectio divina* on the Scripture passage for the day. During this time the Scripture became so empty and flat that one morning I asked the designated reader to please skip the reading and go straight into the silence. For the next four years I lead retreats and workshops, and spoke at Christian events and ministry conventions about a life with God. And all through that time I had no sense of God in me. God remained at the periphery, out of my awareness. I felt empty and lonely and abandoned and helpless. My spiritual practices no longer brought me into the presence of God. I was confused as to my own calling, my spiritual identity, the God I was serving. God became hidden, inaccessible, a silence beyond silence. Not once did I doubt God's existence—I'd had too many profound experiences of God—it was just that God had left, like a man who awakens to find that his beloved wife has packed her things and gone, no note, no forwarding address.

During that time I no longer trusted my own sense of God. I contemplated quitting my job and looking for work in a secular field. I confided my situation to close friends and colleagues. These friends claimed that my work was still effective and important. I remember one colleague telling me, "You may not sense God in what you're teaching, but we do." I learned to lean on these words. My two closest colleagues sat with me each morning in silent prayer, trusting the God I could no longer perceive. I entered into regular spiritual direction. I cancelled many of my speaking engagements, postponed writing projects and greatly reduced my traveling. Over time, gradually, I began to develop a deeper trust in the silent, hidden work of God, work that was no longer subject to my control and manipulation.

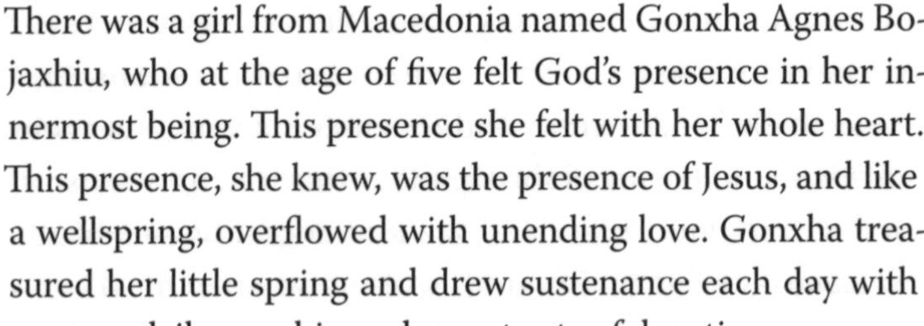

There was a girl from Macedonia named Gonxha Agnes Bojaxhiu, who at the age of five felt God's presence in her innermost being. This presence she felt with her whole heart. This presence, she knew, was the presence of Jesus, and like a wellspring, overflowed with unending love. Gonxha treasured her little spring and drew sustenance each day with prayers, daily worship and secret acts of devotion.

At the age of twelve Gonxha could no longer contain her love for and from Jesus. She needed to find a greater expression of fidelity. Gonxha told her priest of her deep longing to join Jesus in service, in suffering, in saving those whom Jesus loved. At twelve she made a commitment to God to become a missionary and spend her life in service to Jesus. Six years later she was accepted into the Sisters of Loreto, a community committed to poverty, chastity and obedience. With a full and eager heart she left her loving family, her culture, her friendships and all that was familiar in order to serve the One whose presence was warmer than the sun, more nourishing than food. She betrothed herself to Jesus and his suffering amidst the poor. When she made her vows, reports Brian Kolodiejchuk in *Mother Teresa: Come Be My Light*, her name was changed to Teresa.

After years of formation Teresa felt "complete happiness" as "Jesus' little spouse," and was eager to serve God as a teacher in Calcutta. For nine years she endured long hours on her feet—teaching, cooking, cleaning and attending communal prayers within her little mission community. She spent the few hours away from her teaching duties visiting and serving the poor. It was hard work, surrounded by people trapped in unbearable poverty, with few moments for rest—yet Mother Teresa endured all of it happily. The source of her happiness, she wrote to her family, was "the opportunity to imitate Jesus and live in union with Him."

Then on September 10, 1946, at the age of thirty-six, while traveling by train for her annual retreat with her community in Darjeeling, she had a mystical encounter with Jesus in which she heard him say to her, "I thirst." In later years she would expound on this experience as a profound vision of Jesus thirsting on the cross for love, for souls, for companions to share his work and suffering. It was out of this experience that Teresa sensed a deep calling to found the Missionaries of Charity, an order committed to "carry Christ into the homes and streets of the slums, among the sick, dying, the beggars, and the little street children."

For a year following this encounter, Mother Teresa was graced by a series of deep, mystical experiences with Jesus. In these intimate encounters Mother Teresa felt herself being addressed as "my spouse" and "my own little one." In return she called Jesus, "my Jesus" or "my own Jesus." In these conversations she sensed Jesus revealing his heart to her. She sensed his pain, his love, his compassion, his desire for those who suffer. She heard Jesus pleading continually, "Come, come, carry me into the holes of the poor. Come, be my light."

In answer to Jesus' pleading and despite her low status, criticism from other sisters, interior doubts and resistance by her superiors, Mother Teresa did succeed in founding the Missionaries of Charity in 1948. She had finally realized her childhood dream to serve the poorest of the poor.

Then unexpectedly, just one year after founding the Missionaries of Charity, her spirit was plunged into darkness, her prayer became empty and her Jesus, "my own Jesus," went suddenly silent (and would remain silent for the rest of her life). She had given her life to God in trust, in the hope that Jesus would be faithful, present, an attentive companion in the midst of the world's suffering. Jesus became withdrawn, imperceptible, invisible. For the next eleven years Mother Teresa would undergo profound suffering and confusion at the loss of the intimacy of Jesus and the consolations of prayer. For some time her confessor (unaware of Teresa's situation) encouraged her to set aside her spiritual grief and continue to pour herself into her work. She followed his advice, but the inner anguish and loneliness continued. Finally, while on retreat, Mother Teresa spoke with a wise priest who instructed her to express her pain to Jesus. "Write Him," he counseled. "Write Jesus and tell Him of your betrayal, your broken heart, the emptiness that has taken hold of you." So on September 3, 1959, she wrote:

> My own Jesus . . .
>
> They say people in hell suffer eternal pain because of the loss of God—they would go through all that suffering if they had just a little hope of possessing God.—In my soul I feel just that terrible pain of loss—of God not wanting me—of God not being God—of God not really existing (Jesus, please forgive my blasphemies—I have been told to write everything). That darkness that surrounds me on all sides—I can't lift my soul to God—no light or inspiration enters my soul. I speak of love for souls—of tender love for God—words pass through my lips—and I long with a deep longing to believe in them. . . .
>
> In my heart there is no faith—no love—no trust—there is so much pain—the pain of longing, the pain of not being wanted.—I want God with all the powers of my soul—and yet there between us is a terrible separation.—I don't pray any longer—I utter words of community prayers—and try my utmost to get out of every word the sweetness it has to give.—But my

> prayer of union is not there any longer.—I no longer pray.—My soul is not one with You—and yet when alone in the streets I talk to You for hours—of my longing for You.—How intimate are those words—and yet so empty, for they leave me far from You. . . .
>
> I do my best.—I spend myself—but I am more than convinced that the work is not mine. I do not doubt that it was You who called me, with so much love and force.—It was You—I know. . . . [B]ut I have no faith—I don't believe. Jesus, don't let my soul be deceived—nor let me deceive anyone.

Years after her death, biographers have revealed that Mother Teresa's suffering was an experience of the dark night of the soul. The term "dark night of the soul," is a phrase penned by Carmelite John of the Cross in the sixteenth century and does not refer to sin or evil or spiritual apathy. The dark night of the soul is actually a common experience in the Christian life and can occur throughout a person's faith journey. This was the experience that Mother Teresa lived through. This was the same darkness that enclosed me.

God had suddenly become profoundly silent, hidden and inaccessible. Worship, prayer and other spiritual practices no longer delivered the same spiritual consolations I used to receive. My faith practices began to feel useless, at times empty, alienating and even inauthentic. Scripture became flat and unappealing, and the desire to pray or worship seemed to have vanished. During this time I was no longer certain of what I knew of God or even myself. I felt somewhat adrift, unable to control or understand my own spiritual needs. What was most troubling was my inability to authentically express what I was experiencing.

And yet despite the loneliness, despite the silence, I noticed that sin had no appeal. At times I wanted to allow myself to embrace destructive distractions in order to escape my spiritual suffering, but I found my soul resisted these temptations. In the darkness I discovered that despite the lack of any spiritual comfort there remained (illogically) within my soul a blind trust in God. I felt my faith (practices, images, words, understandings) dissipating, and yet at the same time, I had to admit, somehow my faith persisted. Even when I became despondent and tried to let go of faith, still, without encouragement, I noticed my heart waiting for God.

It was a comfort to see this dynamic in Mother Teresa as she went back and forth, claiming she could no longer pray, and yet finding "when alone in the streets—I talk to You for hours—of my longing for You."

Now that those years of darkness have lifted I can reflect on what took place in me during that period. The first and most honest answer is: I don't know. And that seems to be the point. The term *dark night* does not refer to evil or sin, but to a lack of perception. A better translation from the original Spanish would be the "obscure" night of the soul. It's a period in our spiritual journey when God's work in us is obscured, hidden. I now see that during the dark night, God was transforming me in secret, beneath my own knowledge, beneath my own perception, without my own input or management of the process.

This "darkness" was necessary because my images of God, my words for the indescribable presence that we call "God," my theologies and practices were too small and limited. God is mysterious, transcendent, beyond my comprehension. As Augustine once stated, "If you think you've gotten God, it is not God you've gotten." God is simultaneously beyond my ability to grasp and too immanent (closer than my own breathing, my own heartbeat) for me to perceive. As a human being I continually sought a container for God. My spiritual life was an unending attempt to grasp the mystery of God through words, practices, songs, thoughts, feelings, memories and images. Over time I had substituted these symbols of God for the reality of the great "I Am." Over time, my theologies, spiritual practices, experiences of faith, emotional reactions, even my belief statements, had become idols that limited and reduced my awareness of God's presence and possibility.

Similarly, created in the image of God, I had become ignorant of my own potential. It was difficult for me to perceive, much less live from, my innate capacity for love, generosity and compassion. We are created "a little lower than God," and yet I struggled to embody my true nature as God's beloved. Instead, I lived within the confines of the prescribed images and stories given to me by my family and the surrounding culture.

As I grew in faith I had become attached to certain fixed ideas about myself, about the nature of the divine mystery and how we related to one another. I had constructed a faith life that entombed God and myself. Eventually, the great Liberator had to free me from my own constricting faith, my own cherished ideas about the holy Friend, my limited understanding of myself. As Meister Eckhart once wrote when he realized that the God he was serving was too small, my soul "prayed God to rid me of God."

What I have gained through the dark night is to trust my spiritual life to God. Through the dark night I've become less attached to my ideas about God, myself and other people. I hold less tightly to my experiences of success and failure; I've become more aware of my own faults and vulnerabilities, more compassionate toward myself and others.

The experience of the dark night, though painful, can be fruitful in deepening our companionship with Jesus. After eleven years in the dark Mother Teresa trusted her inner suffering to a faithful priest who helped her see that her period of darkness was very similar to the darkness that Jesus experienced on the cross. Once Mother Teresa was able to see this stage of her faith as an invitation into deeper trust and companionship with Jesus' suffering, her anguish was ended and she began a new, more empowered season of life and work. In the dark night she sensed an even deeper solidarity and intimacy with the lonely, the destitute, all who are unseen, unloved and abandoned. She no longer turned to God to give her spiritual visions and consolations, but now accompanied God in the hard work of loving the unloved.

The dark night is a time of liberation, when God weans us from our reliance on spiritual experience, empowering us to no longer live "as servants but as friends." As I embrace the unknowing, as I allow myself to trust that God is in charge of my spiritual life, I have learned to relax, take risks and let go of my anxiety about the future. The experience of the dark night has taught me to be more comfortable in questions, in unknowing, in entering into the lives and situations of people who are in despair, knowing that somehow God is making a way. Through the dark night I am learning, as Mother Teresa learned, to trust others to carry my faith for me. Many times Mother Teresa offered to leave public service, but her sisters and her confessor assured Mother Teresa that although she could not sense her own faith, her life radiated with God's love. Ultimately, the dark night teaches us to trust the hiddenness of God, knowing that our theologies, our practices, and even our experiences of God are limiting.

One of the first Christians to help articulate the dark night was Teresa of Ávila, a companion and mentor to John of the Cross. After living through a period when God felt deeply hidden and silent, Teresa penned this poem to encourage those traveling in the dark:

Let nothing disturb you;
Let nothing make you afraid;
All things pass;
But God is unchanging,
Patience is enough for everything.

PRACTICE

Centering Prayer

Reflection

- Have you ever felt abandoned by God? Like Teresa, write a letter to Jesus or to God expressing your own feelings around this absence. What do you notice is left in you after you pour out your thoughts and feelings? Who is the God who listens to these words?

- Make a list of words and statements that describe the God you no longer believe in. Now see if you can describe, honestly, the God you know at this time in your life. What do you notice about the two lists? How does your sense of self shift in relation to these two descriptions of God?

Action

- There are many forms of prayer in the Christian tradition that invite an "unknowing" or silent trust in the mystery of God. One of those prayer forms is centering prayer. This form of contemplative prayer invites a full opening of mind and heart, soul and body to the Spirit of God (the ultimate mystery that is beyond thoughts, words, images and emotions). In this form of contemplative prayer you are invited to open your awareness to the God who dwells within you—closer than breathing, closer than thinking, closer than consciousness itself.
- Centering prayer invites you to consent to the power of God's presence and unconditional love working within you.
    - Find a quiet place to withdraw to where you will not be disturbed.
    - Before you begin, choose a sacred word to pray with. This word will be a symbol of your intention to be with God. This word expresses your desire to be within God's compassionate presence. Examples include

peace, Jesus, love, trust, shalom, Abba. Once you have selected a word, stick with it. Avoid worrying if some other word might be more "spiritual" and produce "better" results. You word is simply a reminder of your desire to be with God. What matters is your intention to be with God, not your particular word.

- Begin the prayer by sitting in a comfortable, prayerful space. Now close your eyes and settle yourself into God's presence. Take a few breaths and allow yourself to feel a sense of warm hospitality, as if you were waiting to welcome a close friend.
- Begin to silently introduce your sacred word as the symbol of your desire to be open to God's presence. Say the word gently within yourself.
- As your mind wanders into different memories, thoughts and fantasies, simply return to your word as a way of bringing your attention back to God.
- After ten minutes or so, open your eyes and gently return your attention to the room. Close this time of prayer by giving thanks.

- As we live through our own dark nights, we need a spirit of gentleness and self-compassion. The dark night can be a time of loneliness and grief. We need to find others to talk honestly with, particularly people who can hold our interior doubts and suffering. Through the dark night we need others who can sit with us in the silence and uncertainty, people who see God's work in us even when we can't see it. See if you can find a trained spiritual director who will walk with you through this experience. Spiritual directors are not counselors, they are people trained in prayerful listening and discernment. If you do not know of spiritual directors in your area you can find a listing of directors at Spiritual Director's International (sdiworld.org).

10

BUTTERFLIES

The Gift of Death

In three words I can sum up everything
I've learned about life. It goes on.

ROBERT FROST

THE FIRST THING I TRY TO REMEMBER is this: we come from love, and we will return to love. Before parents, before cold and hunger, before color and rhythm and life itself, we were held and created in love. And at the end of our lives, whether death comes calm and peaceful or fearful and tragic, however it comes, at the end, when the last breath escapes, the first thing that will happen is we will let go of the hurt and anxiety and loneliness of this life and return to love.

I was in the room when my father died. It was a hospital room shrouded in dim yellow light, more like a prayer chapel than a critical care unit. My brother, my sister and I had driven four hours through the middle of the night after receiving an urgent phone call. "There's been a terrible accident. Come quickly."

As a practicing Christian I was too familiar with the ways religion is used as a defense—a bulwark from reality, from the truth, from death. I had never been this close to death before. I didn't want to hide from it. I wanted to be with my father in the reality of what he was suffering, no matter how dark or empty. I trusted in God, but not if it kept me from the truth. *Don't spiritualize this,* I said to myself. *Be present to what is real. No pretending. If this is the end, then face the end.* I held my father's hand. I spoke into his ear. I prayed and whispered words of hope to my family. Finally, in the hour just before dawn, the moment came. His weak and erratic heart rate slowed, and then slowed, and then finally stopped.

Some of us dropped our heads and cried; others fell to the floor and wailed—each of us wounded, isolated in our pain. What I remember most, however, was that burrowed way down beneath the tears and wrenching heartache there was a surprising, almost shocking, peace. This deep, undeniable wash of peace ebbed and flowed beneath the hurt, offering a sense of comfort and assurance. It was unquestionable. It was as real as the room, the bed, the gaping grief. Peace. Infinite, unending peace.

One month later I was visiting with my sister. She is not a religious person, and I wondered if her experience at the hospital was similar. "Well, I can tell you one thing," she said. "I'm no longer afraid of death." I looked at her quizzically.

"There was such peace in the room when he died. It was palpable."

A few years later I was talking to my friend Jon about my father's death. Jon works as a hospice chaplain and has seen death up close on many occasions. One spring he was assigned to accompany a middle-aged man named Samuel who was dying of cancer. For six months Jon drove to Samuel's small Craftsman house and spent weekday afternoons visiting and caring for the dying man. Jon enjoyed his time with Samuel, and it wasn't long before they were able to talk with honesty about their lives. One afternoon Jon asked Samuel about the fears he carried in the face of his own death. Samuel shared that although he felt great sorrow, he was not afraid of dying. "I know that God will take care of me," he said plainly.

His greatest fear, he confessed, concerned his sixteen-year-old son. Ever since he'd been diagnosed with cancer, his son, Henri, had become increasingly withdrawn and distant. Samuel confessed, "I worry that this will permanently scar Henri. He's so angry. I've tried to talk with him, but he just stays quiet. Sometimes he can't even look at me. Henri's always been the kind of kid who keeps things to himself. I'm worried he'll fall into a deep depression and won't be able to pull out of it."

Samuel turned to Jon and said, "Can I ask you a favor? Will you try to talk to Henri? Even after I'm gone, will you help him?" Jon promised him that he would.

A few days later, Jon took Henri out for lunch. The meeting was awkward. Jon asked all the tedious questions that adults often ask kids, "How is school? Do you have any hobbies? What do you want to do when you get older?" Visibly depressed, Henri responded with shrugs and one-word answers: "Fine." "No." "Dunno."

After an uneasy silence, Jon told Henri that his parents were worried about him. He asked Henri if he had any questions. Head down and expressionless, Henri gave no reaction. Feeling out of place, Jon said, "Well, if you have any questions you can call me anytime." He handed Henri a card with his phone number. As they stood to leave, Jon looked back and noticed Henri had thrown the card on the floor. Jon drove Henri back to his home. After Jon pulled the car alongside the curb, Henri opened the passenger door, turned back, looked at Jon and said, "I just have one question. How will I know my dad will be okay after he dies?"

Jon thought for a moment, *I don't know. How can anyone know?* But for some reason Jon didn't give this response. Instead, he was surprised to hear himself say with confidence, "You'll know. I'm not sure how. But I promise you, you'll know." The boy studied Jon's face for a moment, then stepped out of the car and walked inside. Immediately, Jon regretted what he'd said. How could he make such a promise? He should have been more careful, more diplomatic, more open-ended.

The weeks passed, Samuel's health deteriorated, and finally in early summer he passed away. Jon was asked to officiate at the graveside service. After the service ended, when all the guests had departed, Jon stood beside the casket with Henri and his mother. Immersed in grief they stood staring silently at the casket, at the bleak, mysterious finality of death. As they stood, a yellow-and-black swallowtail butterfly quietly flew above them and landed at the head of the casket. Still worried about his impulsive promise to Henri, Jon turned to the boy and gestured at the butterfly, as if to say, "Look! See? Here's a sign."

Henri noticed the butterfly and then looked at Jon. Henri's eyes burned with contempt. "A bug lands on my dad's casket and that's supposed to mean something to me? You're pathetic." The boy turned and walked away. His mother, Marion, watched him go. "He's angry," she said to Jon. "He's just angry."

"And I think I've only made things worse," Jon confessed. "I promised he'd know for certain that his dad would be okay after he died. I shouldn't have done that."

The mother put her hand on Jon's back, "I thank you for what you've done for us. He's not your responsibility. I'd appreciate it if you would just say a prayer for Henri now and then." Feeling helpless and embarrassed, Jon nodded his head, hugged the woman and departed.

On the drive home Jon was overwhelmed with despair. He felt like a failure as a chaplain. He was unable to be a comfort to Henri. The boy was right. His gesture at the butterfly was desperate and pathetic. Feeling despondent, Jon did something he rarely did, he began to pray out loud in his car. "God, help Henri. I don't know what to do. Please, God. Please."

Jon drove home praying out of desperation for the grieving boy and his mother. Finally, he arrived at his apartment. He walked inside, but before he could take off his jacket, his cell phone rang. It was Marion.

"Jon?" Her voice was animated.

"Yes."

"Jon, I need you to come over to our house. I need you to come over right now!"

"Is everyone all right?"

"Yes, yes. Everyone is fine. Please, Jon. Just get in your car and drive over as soon as you can."

Jon walked out of his apartment, returned to his car and drove the familiar route to Samuel's house. He walked up the porch and found the front door ajar. He stepped inside. "Hello?" There were sounds coming from the downstairs bedroom, the bedroom where Jon had spent so many afternoons caring for Samuel during the last months of his life.

"Hello!" Jon shouted.

"We're down here!" Marion called out. Jon walked down the stairs, through the hallway, to the room where Samuel died. He carefully swung the door open, stopped and stared in wonder.

The room was filled with butterflies.

Yellow, broad-winged, swallowtail butterflies. There were butterflies gathered on the bed, butterflies airing their wings on the side table, butterflies perched on Marion's shoulders, butterflies fluttering in the air and in and out of the bedroom window that had been propped open just that morning.

Rocking in a chair by his father's bed was Henri. The boy was rocking back and forth, back and forth, laughing and crying, laughing and crying.

Somehow, somewhere deep within me, I trust this story. More than trust. I know this story to be true. It doesn't make sense. My rational mind fails to make the equation work: death is pain and loss. The end. And yet if I glance down within me, there is faith, hope, love and (mystery of all mysteries) joy—unending, unreasonable, foot-stomping joy.

I know it is illogical, but the soul, that which I feel in me (and around me) as soul, knows and trusts and waits for joy. Joy is coming. Joy is here. We come from joy, we return to joy. That is my authority as a spiritual guide, as flimsy as that may seem to the world. It is my knowing and trusting and waiting for this joy that makes me a Christian. Not my seminary studies, not my resume, not my skills in counseling or teaching or preaching, it is this secret, silent voice that says, "Don't fret. Joy is coming." Within my deepest loss and sorrow there persists real trust in life, in people, in God. Something in me waits patiently beneath the hurt and grief, confusion and pain, knowing that eventually I will discover peace. Something in me knows that even amidst the darkest night, there are butterflies, quietly making their way.

PRACTICE

Remembering a Loved One

Reflection

- What do you notice is the shape and character of your faith when you encounter or reflect on the reality of death? What is God like, for you, in the presence of death (absent, present, distant, close)? How does your experience of death inform your own faith? If you knew for certain there is no afterlife, would it change your faith, change how you live?

- Feeling helpless to respond to the boy's hurt and anger, Jon did something he rarely did, he began to pray out loud in his car. "God, help Henri. I don't know what to do. Please, God. Please." In the Jewish tradition, prayers often are full of lament, protest, yearning and desire. Often we don't make contact with these prayers until we recognize our own helplessness. What prayer resides in you in the presence of death? What gives you hope in the midst of death?
- The author writes, "I know it is illogical, but the soul, that which I feel in me (and around me) as soul, knows and trusts and waits for joy. Joy is coming. Joy is here. We come from joy, we return to joy." Do you experience this to be true for you? Do you sense something in you is waiting for joy? What would that joy look like for you, for others?

Action

- Recall a person you have lost. Remember this person's face, voice and what his or her presence felt like. Now take out a piece of paper and write a dialogue between you and the deceased. Begin by writing your own feelings, the things you wish you could say to this person. Then write the name of the person who has died, and after the name write how you imagine this person would respond to the things you have written. Allow yourself to dialogue back and forth as long as it feels right. When you feel finished with the exercise, sit a moment in prayer. Reflect on this exercise with God. What are you being invited to take from this exercise?

Epilogue

The Art of Living

Where do you get that living water?

John 4:11

The first thing you must learn about dowsing is there are no rules.

Richard Webster, *The Art of Dowsing*

I am trying to become a living human being. I am trying to know more fully how to love, grieve, sing, befriend, forgive, heal and give thanks. So often suffering gets in the way. I wish it were not so, and yet all of us inevitably must pass through the shadowlands of doubt and despair. I wish it were not so. But it is so. None of us are exempt. There is only trusting and seeking and failing and then trusting again.

It is the middle of winter 2005, and my wife and I are contemplating buying our first home. The A-frame house is remote, inviting, tucked warmly within the Siskiyou Mountains that climb along the California-Oregon border. The concern is water. The well is undrinkable, toxic with heavy metals. Is it possible to find a clear and constant source of water? We have consulted with neighbors; we have studied geological surveys that map the other wells in the valley. And still, we have yet to find water within the granite- and shale-covered land. A local who has lived in the area for years hears of our situation and tells me, "You need a dowser, a diviner, if you're going to find water."

I am skeptical. More than skeptical. As a person of faith, I am alert to superstition. But dead-ends convince me to give it a try. On a cold February morning, with the wind spitting ice and snow, a battered station wagon pulls up to the property and out walks an elderly man of seventy-plus years. He stands in a worn Chevron Gas baseball cap, a baby-blue windbreaker his only protection against the elements. The man, we have been informed, is mostly deaf, his speech thick and rounded, difficult to decipher by the untrained ear. He has brought his own interpreter, his middle-aged daughter, dressed more appropriately in wool hat, scarf, gloves and down jacket. The woman greets us and then explains how we will proceed. "Dad is going to walk the property with these two copper wires. You're welcome to walk with him and ask questions. I'll communicate for you." The wind is sharp and brittle. My face burns in the icy cold. But the dowser, the diviner, holds his arms outstretched, his bare hands out, two three-foot lengths of stiff wire held between his fingers. Immediately I think of carnival barkers and street-corner con men. The whole ritual feels like an act—maybe an act the man believes in, but nevertheless a conjuring.

For the next thirty minutes I walk alongside the dowser through the brutal cold, up and down the five-acre property. From time to time he stops and speaks with slurred and heavy sounds. His daughter interprets: "He says the water runs deep. He says there is lots of iron in the water, not drinkable. He says there is little water on this side of the property." I listen and nod and kick myself for agreeing to pay this man for the obvious. We walk until my face is cold and chapped from the wind. I cannot understand how the dowser's hands have not gone numb. Then suddenly, the wires cross and fall toward the ground, the man speaks excitedly, and the daughter says, "Here. He says the water is strong here. A clear stream. It's deep and it's potable. Nine hundred feet down. Right here." From somewhere inside her thick coat the daughter produces a wooden stake with a red ribbon tied to the top. The ground frozen, she lays the marker on its side. "Right here. This is the spot."

Weeks go by. I spend many moments staring at the dowser's marking, but eventually the risk and expense overcome hope and we pass on the home. Late that summer I encounter our realtor in a coffee shop. He has just sold the mountain property. The buyers hired a geologist and drilled for water at the exact spot that the dowser had marked. "Did they find water?" I ask. "Yes they did. At 910 feet. Clear and clean. Just as the dowser said." I listen and wonder at the man who knew where water could be found, and then feel the great living depth of all that I do not know.

As I reflect on this experience I realize it is possible that the man and his daughter had studied the depths of other wells in the area or perhaps had seen a geological survey. It is also possible the man had some other knowing, some other experience, some connection to the earth, some intuition, some hope. It is up to me to choose which story to believe, and the stories I choose to believe alter the way I live.

"Choose life, not death" is the ancient and holy and simple instruction for sorting what should be kept and what should be discarded. We all get to choose. One of the great Christian "sorters," a true doctor of the human soul, was Ignatius of Loyola. Ignatius's great art was discernment—the prayerful process of sifting through our human experience in a way that helps us see where life is blocked or opening up. One of Ignatius's great tools is a little prayer called "the Examen," in which he invites a seeker to pray over their day, noticing the moments when grace—life, love, creativity, the Spirit—broke through. Ignatius then asks a person to pray through their day a second time with the purpose of naming and holding moments of lifelessness—moments when one felt stuck, anxious, dry, isolated, closed off to God's love. The reason Ignatius asks people to pray over their experience a second time is because he knew that in order to locate the living water of God we must not only hold what is life-giving but also what is hollow and burdensome. Both experiences are fruitful, helping us understand where to direct the heart's attention.

Most of us have not been encouraged to trust life's difficulties. We have not been equipped, given a divining rod, to seek water beneath the hard experiences that life brings us. We have not been given permission to name and hold and sift through what is deadening to us personally and communally. Yet in my own spiritual life it has been through trusting these very moments of absence and emptiness that I have received the greatest spiritual insight and freedom. Over time I have learned that if I can stay with the discomfort, the absence, the hurt, the grief (often only through the help of others), these hard experiences can soften my heart, expand my vision and open me to a new awareness of the deep truths of God.

But not always.

Sometimes the hard things in life bring nothing but ruin. Sometimes burnout leads to depression. Sometimes injustice leads to violence. Sometimes brokenness leads to self-hatred. Sometimes doubt leads to a loss of faith. Sometimes death removes all hope. There are hard things and there are harder things.

The good news (although it may not sound that way) is that every once in a while we get a little space, a little quiet, a little distance from the suffering. Sometimes a friend comes by the house. Sometimes Jesus writes in the sand and distracts us from the shame. Sometimes the hermit thrush sings outside our window and we sense a moment. A moment when we are no longer enmeshed in what ails us. A moment of freedom. A moment when we get to choose. Even when we are cornered by terrible pain, still, sometimes freedom rises up in us and we get to choose. We get to choose whether our helplessness draws us toward or away from prayer. We get to choose whether our grief deepens our empathy or sours us into resentment. We get to choose whether to allow the difficulties we have suffered to break or expand us.

And if we are able to listen for life, if we are able to tilt our ear toward the frozen ground, if we are willing to be honest about the pain, sometimes there is a gift in what we have been given. Sometimes the veil of tears lifts. Sometimes, our suffering can be redeemed and made useful, our torn heart suddenly opened into a passageway for receiving and returning love.

What is needed is an instrument, a divining rod of sorts, a willingness to listen to our own searching soul, the very place that senses water deep beneath the hard shale and granite—that place in us where God dwells. And if we are listening, if we are open, we might find grace where we least expect it: A kiss on the cheek in Maddalena's kitchen, a smiling wise man in a federal prison, a cheering husband at a graduation ceremony, a comforting hand from a woman in black, a widow's embrace in the midst of a terrible wrong. Living is an art, and there are no formulas, no designated methods for dealing with hard things. There is only the waiting and the listening and the dancing when life springs forth.

Acknowledgments

My gratitude to the editors who first solicited some of the material in this book, particularly Martin Saunders and Ruth Mawhinney. My thanks (and apologies?) to fellow travelers Mark Montgomery and Paul Chambers. Thank you to Cindy Bunch and folks at InterVarsity Press for assistance in preparing the text. Heartfelt gratitude for counsel and suggestions from oldest and dearest friend Kirk Wulf. My understanding of the inner life and how we approach difficult emotions has been deeply formed by my friend and former colleague Frank Rogers. Careful readers will feel his influence in some of the practices.

My greatest spiritual teacher and the person most responsible for my capacity to love and forgive and create is my wife, the love of my life, Jill Catton Yaconelli. Thank you for spending countless hours editing, reflecting and discussing each of these chapters with me. This book would not exist without your love and careful reading. Thank you, sweetheart.

Did you know that SPCK is a registered charity?

As well as publishing great books by leading Christian authors, we also . . .

. . . make assemblies meaningful and fun for over a million children by running www.assemblies.org.uk, a popular website that provides free assembly scripts for teachers. For many children, school assembly is the only contact they have with Christian faith and culture, and the only time in their week for spiritual reflection.

. . . help prisoners to become confident readers with our easy-to-read stories. Poor literacy is a huge barrier to rehabilitation. Prisoners identify with the believable heroes of our gritty fiction. At the same time, questions at the end of each chapter help them to examine their choices from a moral perspective and to build their reading confidence.

. . . support student ministers overseas in their training through partnerships in the Global South.

Please support these great schemes: visit www.spck.org.uk/support-us to find out more.